Robert R. Nelson
Editor

Past President and CEO
National Restaurant Association
Past President and CEO
American Hotel & Lodging Association

"**S**TRONGLY RECOMMENDED. This is THE MOST COMPREHENSIVE anthology of research and analysis in convention and exhibition facility development in the history of the industry. Dr. Nelson and the contributors to this valuable resource have provided the history, data, trends, political, social, and even environmental framework for critical decision-making. The level of research, while rigorous, is also very approachable for professionals at every level. Organizations in search of new economic development opportunities through convention and exhibition facility development will greatly benefit from this comprehensive tool."

Dr. Joe Goldblatt, CSEP
Professor and Executive Director
for Professional Development
& Strategic Partnerships
School of Tourism
and Hospitality Management
Temple University

"**W**ILL HELP EVERY COMMUNITY UNDERSTAND WHAT IS NEEDED FOR A SUCCESSFUL CONVENTION BUSINESS, the realities of the market and the inter-city competition for meetings, and the community planning activities that must precede any decision to invest in a convention center. Community leaders need to understand the dimensions of the public/private partnership required for a successful convention center, and this book is the first step along the path to building the facility that is actually needed while understanding the pitfalls, challenges, and obstacles in making a community's meetings business a success."

Mark S. Rosentraub, PhD
Dean
Levin College of Urban Affairs
Cleveland State University

More pre-publication
REVIEWS, COMMENTARIES, EVALUATIONS . . .

"A WONDERFUL COLLECTION. . . . This combination of practical concepts, cases, and advice on convention center tourism should be REQUIRED READING for anyone considering such projects. The book includes the diverse perspectives of a variety of experts in public policy, tourism convention management, and urban planning. The lessons and insights of the experts featured in these pages provide a COMPREHENSIVE AND BALANCED treatment of current issues."

Cathy A. Enz, PhD
Co-Author of Hospitality
Strategic Management
and American Lodging Excellence
and the Lewis G. Schaeneman, Jr.
Professor of Innovation
and Dynamic Management
Cornell University School
of Hotel Administration

The Haworth Hospitality Press®
An Imprint of The Haworth Press, Inc.

New York • London • Victoria (AU)
www.HaworthPress.com

Current Issues
in Convention
and Exhibition Facility
Development

Current Issues in Convention and Exhibition Facility Development
has been co-published simultaneously as *Journal of Convention &*
Event Tourism, Volume 6, Numbers 1/2 2004.

The *Journal of Convention & Event Tourism*™ Monographic "Separates" (formerly the *Journal of Convention & Exhibition Management*

Below is a list of "separates," which in serials librarianship means a special issue simultaneously published as a special journal issue or double-issue *and* as a "separate" hardbound monograph. (This is a format which we also call a "DocuSerial.")

"Separates" are published because specialized libraries or professionals may wish to purchase a specific thematic issue by itself in a format which can be separately cataloged and shelved, as opposed to purchasing the journal on an on-going basis. Faculty members may also more easily consider a "separate" for classroom adoption.

"Separates" are carefully classified separately with the major book jobbers so that the journal tie-in can be noted on new book order slips to avoid duplicate purchasing.

You may wish to visit Haworth's Website at . . .

http://www.HaworthPress.com

. . . to search our online catalog for complete tables of contents of these separates and related publications.

You may also call 1-800-HAWORTH (outside US/Canada: 607-722-5857), or Fax 1-800-895-0582 (outside US/Canada: 607-771-0012), or e-mail at:

docdelivery@haworthpress.com

Current Issues in Convention and Exhibition Facility Development, edited by Robert R. Nelson, PhD (Vol. 6, Numbers 1/2 2004). *"MUST READING for travel and tourism industry leaders and students." (William P. Fisher, PhD, Past President and CEO, National Restaurant Association; Past President and CEO, American Hotel & Lodging Association)*

Current Issues
in Convention
and Exhibition Facility
Development

Robert R. Nelson, PhD
Editor

Current Issues in Convention and Exhibition Facility Development
has been co-published simultaneously as *Journal of Convention &*
Event Tourism, Volume 6, Numbers 1/2 2004.

The Haworth Hospitality Press®
An Imprint of The Haworth Press, Inc.

New York • London • Victoria (AU)
www.HaworthPress.com

Published by

The Haworth Hospitality Press®, 10 Alice Street, Binghamton, NY 13904-1580 USA

The Haworth Hospitality Press® is an imprint of The Haworth Press, Inc., 10 Alice Street, Binghamton, NY 13904-1580 USA.

Current Issues in Convention and Exhibition Facility Development has been co-published simultaneously as *Journal of Convention & Event Tourism,* Volume 6, Numbers 1/2 2004.

The development, preparation, and publication of this work has been undertaken with great care. However, the publisher, employees, editors, and agents of The Haworth Press and all imprints of The Haworth Press, Inc., including The Haworth Medical Press® and The Pharmaceutical Products Press®, are not responsible for any errors contained herein or for consequences that may ensue from use of materials or information contained in this work. Opinions expressed by the author(s) are not necessarily those of The Haworth Press, Inc.

Cover design by Marylouise Doyle

Library of Congress Cataloging-in-Publication Data

Current issues in convention and exhibition facility development / Robert R. Nelson, editor.
      p. cm.

   "Current Issues in Convention and Exhibition Facility Development has been co-published simultaneously as Journal of Convention & Event Tourism, Volume 6, Numbers 1/2 2004."
   Includes bibliographical references and index.
   ISBN 0-7890-2597-3 (hard cover : alk. paper) – ISBN 0-7890-2598-1 (soft cover : alk. paper)
   1. Convention facilities. 2. Congresses and conventions. 3. Exhibition buildings. I. Nelson, Robert R. (Robert Richard), 1961-

TX911.2.C87 2004
647'.9691–dc22
                                                                                            2004001418

Indexing, Abstracting & Website/Internet Coverage

Journal of Convention & Event Tourism

This section provides you with a list of major indexing & abstracting services. That is to say, each service began covering this periodical during the year noted in the right column. Most Websites which are listed below have indicated that they will either post, disseminate, compile, archive, cite or alert their own Website users with research-based content from this work. (This list is as current as the copyright date of this publication.)

Abstracting, Website/Indexing Coverage . . . . Year When Coverage Began

- *Academic Search: data base of 2,000 selected academic serials, updated monthly: EBSCO Publishing* **2003**

- *Business Source Corporate: coverage of nearly 3,350 quality magazines and journals; designed to meet the diverse information needs of corporations; EBSCO Publishing <http://www.ciret-tourism.com>* **2003**

- *CIRET (Centre International de Recherches et d'Etudes Touristiques). Computerized Touristique & General Bibliography) <http://www.ciret-tourism.com>* **2000**

- *CNPIEC Reference Guide: Chinese National Directory of Foreign Periodicals* **1998**

- *Hospitality and Tourism Index (EBSCO)* **2003**

- *Lodging, Restaurant & Tourism Index* **1998**

- *Management & Marketing Abstracts* **1998**

- *National Criminal Justice Reference Service <http://www.ncjrs.org>* **1998**

- *Nutrition Abstracts & Reviews, Series A, Human & Experimental (% CAB Intl/CAB ACCESS) <http://www.cabi.org>* **1998**

(continued)

*Special bibliographic notes related to special journal issues
(separates) and indexing/abstracting:*

- indexing/abstracting services in this list will also cover material in any "separate" that is co-published simultaneously with Haworth's special thematic journal issue or DocuSerial. Indexing/abstracting usually covers material at the article/chapter level.
- monographic co-editions are intended for either non-subscribers or libraries which intend to purchase a second copy for their circulating collections.
- monographic co-editions are reported to all jobbers/wholesalers/approval plans. The source journal is listed as the "series" to assist the prevention of duplicate purchasing in the same manner utilized for books-in-series.
- to facilitate user/access services all indexing/abstracting services are encouraged to utilize the co-indexing entry note indicated at the bottom of the first page of each article/chapter/contribution.
- this is intended to assist a library user of any reference tool (whether print, electronic, online, or CD-ROM) to locate the monographic version if the library has purchased this version but not a subscription to the source journal.
- individual articles/chapters in any Haworth publication are also available through the Haworth Document Delivery Service (HDDS).

Current Issues in Convention and Exhibition Facility Development

CONTENTS

ABOUT THE EDITOR

Robert R. Nelson, PhD, is Associate Professor and Director of Undergraduate Studies at the University of Delaware's Department of Hotel, Restaurant & Institutional Management. Dr. Nelson is widely published in the area of tourism and economic development. He is a graduate of Cornell's School of Hotel Administration and has an MBA from Drexel University. He received his PhD from the University of Delaware's School of Urban Affairs and Public Policy, where his dissertation topic was "Convention Centers as Catalysts for Local Economic Development."

Introduction

This special volume provides multi-disciplinary perspectives on convention and exposition facility development. The questions surrounding facility development and expansion are becoming increasingly important as the number of centers continues to grow throughout the world. The growth in the number and size of modern convention facilities is understandable. The potential benefits of convention trade to local economies are well documented. Judd (1988, p. 382) called the tourism and convention trade "one of the most important facets of central business district economics." Bramberger and Parham (1984), Braum (1992), Dwyer (2002), Fenich (1992 and 1994), Law (1993) and Rodgers (1988) are among the many whose studies have found that while convention centers typically lose money on operations, they provide net economic gains for the larger community. Crouch and Ritchie (1998, p. 49) go beyond the economic issues and note that the "meetings and convention industry worldwide has grown to become a significant economic, political, and social phenomenon."

Communities looking to develop convention centers face a wide range of questions, including should the center be built at all, how might it be financed, and who will be responsible for marketing and operating the facility? In the opening piece of this volume, J. Dana Clark draws on his considerable industry and academic experience to present ten critical questions that communities confront when considering convention center projects. Clark's piece offers clear, practical advice for communities considering convention center development.

Richard G. McNeill and Ronald A. Evans follow with more guidance in their article "So You Want to Build a Convention Center: The Case of Hope versus Reality." They provide a "road map" to direct convention center development and apply it to a case study in Flagstaff, Arizona. This project involves a complex three-way partnership that includes the public and private sectors

[Haworth co-indexing entry note]: "Introduction." Nelson, Robert R. Co-published simultaneously in *Journal of Convention & Event Tourism* (The Haworth Hospitality Press, an imprint of The Haworth Press, Inc.) Vol. 6, No. 1/2, 2004, pp. 1-4; and: *Current Issues in Convention and Exhibition Facility Development* (ed: Robert R. Nelson) The Haworth Hospitality Press, an imprint of The Haworth Press, Inc., 2004, pp. 1-4. Single or multiple copies of this article are available for a fee from The Haworth Document Delivery Service [1-800-HAWORTH, 9:00 a.m. - 5:00 p.m. (EST). E-mail address: docdelivery@haworthpress.com].

Digital Object Identifier: 10.1300/J452v06n01_01

working along with Northern Arizona University. This example illustrates a creative approach to facility development involving many stakeholders with different goals.

Carlsen follows with a case study from the opposite side of the globe. He uses the design and development of the Perth Convention and Exhibition Center to examine the economic, political, and social issues raised by facility development. This case study illustrates the complex and often highly politicized processes that go into developing public-private partnerships used to bring convention center projects to fruition.

In their article, "Casinos and Conventions: Strange Bedfellows," George G. Fenich and Kathryn Hashimoto describe a fairly new trend in convention and exhibition facility: the casino industry is encouraging and developing convention centers. Until fairly recently, casinos reserved their rooms for hard core gamblers. Fenich and Hashimoto chronicle how the spread of legalized gambling in the United States from its traditional base of Las Vegas has created a more competitive environment that has forced casinos to look for new ways to fill their hotel rooms and gaming tables. Meetings and conventions are emerging as an important market for the gaming industry. Today, casinos are playing a major role in convention center development in the United States.

In "Convention Center Wars and the Decline of Local Democracy" David H. Laslo and Dennis R. Judd argue that decision making processes regarding public investments in convention centers are increasingly moving in a direction that weakens any opposition to these projects. Laslo and Judd acknowledge that conventions, meetings, and business travel play a major role in local economic vitality and revitalization of central business districts. However, they are critical of decision making processes that limit public debate and circumvent democratic processes. They use St. Louis as an illustrative case study that they claim is typical of decision making processes used to limit opposition and debate regarding the use public money to build and expand convention facilities.

Heywood T. Sanders' "Convention Mythology" provides a cautionary note to those considering developing or expanding convention facilities. He chronicles the convention center development boom in the United States and warns of a series of "convention myths" that have fueled this growth in convention space. Sanders presents convincing empirical evidence to refute exaggerated claims of convention and tradeshow industry growth. He goes on to provide critical analyses of specific feasibility studies used to promote the use of public funds for convention center development projects. This hard-hitting piece is sure to spark discussion and debate.

The final piece, "The City as a Destination: Measuring Its Attractiveness," presents a model to help communities assess their potential attractiveness as convention destinations. The author, David C. Petersen, is a highly sought-after town planning consultant and the author of *Developing Sports, Convention, and Performing Arts Centers*. In this article, Petersen concludes that convention centers are not a panacea that will work for every community. He offers the "mix-mass-mesh" model as a framework that communities can use to evaluate their attractiveness as convention destinations. This thought provoking model points to the need for further research to help objectively assess the likelihood that a given convention center development project is likely to be competitive in a crowded marketplace.

In an attempt to provide a variety of perspectives on the subject of convention facility development, this volume includes submissions from a range of disciplines including public policy, tourism, convention management, and urban planning. All of the authors in this volume are widely published in their own fields, but their diverse perspectives on convention and exhibition facility development have never before been brought together within the pages of a single publication. Hopefully this volume will encourage further cross fertilization of ideas across academic and professional disciplines regarding this important topic.

This editor is highly indebted to all those who responded to the initial call for papers and especially to the final authors who were so responsive to editorial comments. Further gratitude must go to the many reviewers who contributed to this issue. Finally, special thanks go to the assistant editor, Lynette Arceneaux. Without her thorough and tireless work, this issue would have never made it to print.

Robert R. Nelson, PhD
Department of Hotel
Restaurant & Institutional Management
University of Delaware

REFERENCES

Bramberger, R. T., & Parham, D. W. (1984, November). Indianapolis's economic development strategy. *Urban Land*, 12-18.

Braum, B. M. (1992). The economic contributions of conventions: The case of Orlando, Florida. *Journal of Travel Research, 30*(3), 32-37.

Crouch, G. I., & Ritchie, J. R. B. (1998). Convention site selection research: A review, conceptual model, and propositional framework. *Journal of Convention & Exhibition Management, 1*(1), 49-69.

Dwyer, L. (2002). Economic contribution of convention tourism: Conceptual and empirical issues. In K. Weber & K. Chon (Eds.), *Convention tourism: International research and industry perspectives* (pp. 21-35). New York: The Haworth Press, Inc.

Fenich, G. G. (1992). *The dollars and sense of convention centers* (Doctoral dissertation, Rutgers University, East Brunswick, NJ).

Fenich, G. G. (1994). An assessment of whether the convention center in New York is successful as a tool for economic development. *Economic Development Quarterly, 8*(3), 245-255.

Judd, D. R. (1988). *The politics of American cities* (3rd ed.). Glenview, IL: Scott, Foresman and Co.

Law, C. M. (1993). *Urban tourism: Attracting visitors to large cities.* London: Mansell.

Considering a Convention Center:
Ten Questions Communities Will Confront

J. Dana Clark, BA, MBA, PhD

[Future]

SUMMARY. An increasing number of communities are actively considering the construction of a convention center. Rather than being a 1-step, build or not build process, the convention center decision process is multi-stepped. Many of the decisions that must be made in the process are complicated and have huge potential implications for existing lodging facilities and other industry and non-industry players. Further, because the process includes numerous steps, the entire process is often very time-consuming. The author used a variety of sources to suggest the elements that should be considered when thinking about the construction of a modern convention center for a community. *[Article copies available for a fee from The Haworth Document Delivery Service: 1-800-HAWORTH. E-mail address: <docdelivery@haworthpress.com> Website: <http://www.HaworthPress. com> © 2004 by The Haworth Press, Inc. All rights reserved.]*

KEYWORDS. Convention center, convention bureau, outsourcing, booking policies, center marketing

---

J. Dana Clark is Former President of the Travel Council of North Carolina, Former Vice-President of Convention Development for the Charlotte Convention and Visitors Bureau, and Associate Professor of Management, Appalachian State University, Department of Management, P.O. Box 32033, Boone, NC 28608-2033 (E-mail: clarkjd@appstate.edu).

[Haworth co-indexing entry note]: "Considering a Convention Center: Ten Questions Communities Will Confront." Clark, J. Dana. Co-published simultaneously in *Journal of Convention & Event Tourism* (The Haworth Hospitality Press, an imprint of The Haworth Press, Inc.) Vol. 6, No. 1/2, 2004, pp. 5-21; and: *Current Issues in Convention and Exhibition Facility Development* (ed: Robert R. Nelson) The Haworth Hospitality Press, an imprint of The Haworth Press, Inc., 2004, pp. 5-21. Single or multiple copies of this article are available for a fee from The Haworth Document Delivery Service [1-800-HAWORTH, 9:00 a.m. - 5:00 p.m. (EST). E-mail address: docdelivery@haworthpress.com].

http://www.haworthpress.com/web/JCET
© 2004 by The Haworth Press, Inc. All rights reserved.
Digital Object Identifier: 10.1300/J452v06n01_02

More and more cities find themselves in the position of studying the feasibility of building a convention center as part of their tourism infrastructure. The study process from beginning to end can take 10 years (Mann, 2000) or more and is often an emotional roller-coaster for many of the stakeholders involved. About the time one major question is answered, another two or three seem to pop up.

Convention centers are built for a variety of reasons. Further, convention centers are built with a variety of attributes depending upon what a community foresees as the building's mission or missions.

At first, communities simply felt their way through the process, confronting each major question or problem as it came along. Now, though, we have 30 or more years of experience from which to draw. Some patterns have emerged and there is now some predictability to the study process.

According to Rutherford (1990):

> Because of the economic impact of conventions on host communities in the last 15 [to] 20 years, there has been a veritable explosion in the building of special-purpose facilities designed to make the planning and execution of conventions and tradeshows convenient and attractive to their managers and attendees.

In the beginning, these special-purpose facilities were built primarily in larger cities. However, as the economic impacts became better understood, cities of varying size have entered or are considering entering the market. PricewaterhouseCoopers, in their *Convention Center Annual Report* (1999, 2000, 2001), now classifies a city's market by number of hotel rooms. This has yielded three types of cities (in this case, all in North America):

- Gateway cities–Metro areas with more than 25,000 total hotel rooms (PricewaterhouseCoopers, 1999).
- National cities–Metro areas with 15,000 to 25,000 hotel rooms (PricewaterhouseCoopers, 2000).
- Regional cities–Metro areas with fewer than 15,000 hotel rooms (PricewaterhouseCoopers, 2001).

WHY CITIES CONSIDER BUILDING A CONVENTION CENTER

Why do cities consider building convention centers in the first place? The biggest reason is usually economic impact. According to the *Convention Income Survey Report* (2000) published by the International Association of

Convention and Visitor Bureaus Foundation, conventioneers, tradeshow delegates, and association officials spend a considerable amount of money when in a community for a convention. This ranges from $579 to $739 per delegate, per event, or $222 to $277 per delegate, per day, depending upon the role the participant is playing. Multiply this by average length of stays of 2.54 nights to 3.55 nights and the figures truly start to add up. It should be noted that these figures vary greatly from city to city.

Further, according to the same study, the money is really spread around in host communities. Dollars are not simply spent in hotels and restaurants, but at museums, theaters, sporting events, retail stores, and other local businesses.

Shows can be of considerable size. A study by the International Association of Exhibition Management (as cited in Vasos, 2000) looked at how big average attendance was at shows held by their members. An average consumer show had 55,000 attendees. Other shows listed with attendees included food shows (15,500), education shows (9,000), computer shows (14,000), and manufacturing shows (10,000). Couple these attendance figures with spending per delegate, and a huge economic impact picture begins to emerge.

As we will see, there are other reasons for building convention centers. However, the number one reason for building such a building is to positively impact the community from an economic perspective.

There is no question that hotels and motels are perceived as the big winners in the process. It is perceived that building a convention center will improve business for local lodging establishments. There is no doubt that the total number of room nights in the city will improve with the building of a center. Reyn Bowman, the head of the Convention and Visitors Bureau in Durham, North Carolina, was quick to point out, however, that this is true "only if marketing

TABLE 1. Ten Convention Center Questions

1.	(If we build a convention center) How will we define success?
2.	Should we build a convention center?
3.	How will a new center be financed?
4.	How will we get permission from the local citizens to build a center?
5.	Where will the new center be located?
6.	Who will market the building?
7.	Who will manage the building?
8.	What will be the center's booking policies?
9.	Who will provide services in the building?
10.	What design elements should be included in a center?

and promotions are increased and if they have a very well established and competitive CVB. The building (of a convention center) in and of itself will not make the community competitive (in the meetings market)" (personal communication, May 20, 2002; May 24, 2002).

Over time, building new centers makes a community more attractive to firms considering building a hotel there. Often, however, a new center means new hotels; thus, in the long run, city-wide occupancy really is not improved all that much, though, again, total lodging revenues do increase as do occupancy tax collections.

TEN CONVENTION CENTER QUESTIONS

This paradigm is based upon dozens of interviews with city officials, convention center managers, convention bureau officials, and a review of what has been written on the subject in a wide variety of publications. Further, the author has worked through a number of studies while employed in various hospitality positions and has consulted on the topic for many years. Finally, a rough draft of the study was mailed to over a dozen hospitality representatives who have knowledge of the topic. Their comments were reviewed and incorporated into the paper.

(If we build a convention center) How will we define success?

It is always interesting to listen to local officials describing a convention center as being a "success." Success may be rightfully claimed in a number of ways, yet depending upon one's point of view, another person might look at the same building and describe it as a failure. It is important from the beginning that various stakeholders understand that success may be defined in a number of ways, including:

1. The building is profitable–Convention centers are almost never profitable. They are viewed in most cities as a loss leader to get conventioneers into a town to spend money. If centers made money, private companies, rather than governments, would build them.
2. The center covers its operating expenses–Even this is hard to do given the competitive nature of the business, the size of the buildings, and the number of people it takes to operate one. Cities have become so aggressive in booking business it is very hard for a center to charge rates that even cover operating expenses.

3. The center serves as an economic catalyst–As can be derived from the figures already presented, most centers can be described as a success from this perspective. Once an accurate multiplier is added, a real case for success can be made here. It is important that the community and its leaders understand this concept from the beginning. It is also important for the hospitality industry to tell this story over and over again to the citizenry.

4. The center serves as a community center–Centers often serve as a place for a community to gather for special events. These events may include graduations, balls, galas, weddings and others. It may be wise for a community to consider calling one of these buildings a "civic center" as the building is almost always successful in this function. The center serves as a community's "living room."

5. PricewaterhouseCoopers' *2000 Convention & Congress Center Annual Report*–In a survey they report a center's success is measured by (in North America):

- (Lodging) Room nights generated–85%.
- Economic impact–81%.
- Number of events–62%.
- Building occupancy–58%.
- Attendance–50%.
- Taxes generated–50%.
- Availability for local events–42%.
- Other–12%.

While this report is very useful, it must be remembered that the figures represent a survey of center officials in cities where centers already exist.

Should we build a convention center?

There are such a variety of detailed questions that have to be answered, that this question simply goes beyond what can be covered here. However, some of the basics include:

1. Is there a community development plan, and where does a center fit into this plan?
2. Is a center the best way to positively impact the community if it is being used for economic development?
3. Is there a need locally, regionally, and so forth?
4. Are there identifiable markets for the building?
5. Who will the local enemies be, and why will they oppose the building? Reasons may include traffic congestion, higher taxes, priorities, and so forth.

6. Can the building generate enough revenue so as not to be too big a drain on government coffers?

How will a new center be financed?

It seems that most convention centers use some unique collection of funding sources to make a building work financially. The Oregon Convention Center is a typical example (Blosser, 1996). They used "layered" taxes–including property taxes, state lottery taxes, and a one time, city LID tax–to finance their center.

1. The International Association of Assembly Managers provided an article (Blosser, 1996) listing a wide variety of possible funding sources, including:

   - Hotel/Motel (lodging) taxes.
   - Food and beverage taxes.
   - Rental car taxes.
   - Revenue bonds.
   - General obligation bonds.
   - Tax increment financing.
   - Sales tax.
   - Lottery funds.
   - Entertainment (or admission) tax.
   - Special district tax.
   - General funds.

2. Some specific funding examples (Dobrian, 2000) include:

   - Pittsburgh, Pennsylvania: A local referendum failed. They were able to get $150 million from state government plus a 1% hotel and general sales tax increase.
   - Portland, Oregon: Voters wanted to expand the center but not be taxed. They increased hotel and rental car taxes by 2.5% each.
   - Syracuse, New York: They got a $40 million grant from the state and bonded $30 million from the county.
   - Charleston, South Carolina: They expanded their civic center with $9 million funded with two revenue bonds.
   - Madison, Wisconsin: Funded by revenue bonds, the state built and operates the parking lot, and $9 million was provided from private donations.

- According to Chuck Jones, director of the Athens (Georgia) Convention and Visitors Bureau, Athens has and is using SPLOST (Special Purpose Local Option Sales Tax) in a variety of ways. This 1% local option tax has been used to build the Classic Center in Athens and is now being used to build an adjoining parking deck (personal communication, May 22, 2002).

Suffice it to say that each community must come up with a funding plan that will successfully function in the situation the community is working with.

How will we get permission from the local citizens to build a center?

1. In most communities, some sort of public funding will be needed. That implies that some sort of voter approval will be necessary before building can begin. It is one thing to find a funding source, but quite another to get voters to approve using those funds to build a convention center. By and large, the average voter understands arenas, performing arts centers, stadiums, schools, courthouses, and the like. Convention centers, however, are not widely understood by the average citizen. Steve Camp (personal communication, May 15, 2002), who heads both the convention and visitors bureau and the convention center in Columbia, South Carolina, has said, "A convention center is the hardest thing to sell to a community." Those trying to get a center built will usually have to answer the following questions at this point:

   - Who will get the community behind this effort?
   - How should the public relations campaign be handled?
   - Who will get the necessary politicians on board?
   - What will the message be?

2. An article from IAAM suggests the following points when putting together a successful campaign:

   - Form a Blue Ribbon Committee.
   - Raise campaign funds if necessary.
   - Hire a public relations/strategy firm to direct and staff the committee efforts.
   - Get hospitality board and government leaders on the area speakers' bureaus to meet the public to explain the project and why it is important.
   - Structure all pertinent information in layman's terms so it is easily understood and not confusing to voters.

- Stop around the community to all the civic groups possible.
- Bring the campaign to the voting public.
- Perform polling surveys throughout the process.

3. Other possibilities–Occasionally a community can find a way to not take the question directly to voters. In Charlotte, North Carolina, the industry got permission to build a center by simply getting a positive vote from the city council.

Where will the new center be located?

This is one of the most controversial questions to be answered in the whole process. A number of stakeholders will make powerful cases for locating a center in one place or another for a variety of reasons. Too often local lodging facilities–who pay occupancy taxes that, in essence, pay for the center–work for years to get approval to build a center only to lose the battle over where the center is located. As pointed out by William Overfelt, general manager of the Knoxville Convention Center, hotels simply collect the occupancy tax but do not pay it (personal communication, May 16, 2002). While this is true, many hotels psychologically feel they are paying the occupancy tax. A center not located close to existing lodging facilities results in these very facilities financing the catalyst building that is the powerful base for new competition; namely, new hotels built close to the new center. If existing lodging facilities cannot win this battle, there is little reason for them to support the building of a new center. It is possible to build a new convention center and have city-wide occupancy figures actually go down. A variety of building sites have been considered by cities, including:

1. Close to the current hotel/restaurant infrastructure–Meeting and show planners prefer convention centers located close to hotels and restaurants. "Close" is usually defined as being within two or three blocks. Building a center too far away from necessary infrastructure will make selling the new center very difficult. Existing lodging facilities need to play a big role when site location is being determined. A wise thought at this point is to bring in meeting and show planners and ask them where they would like a center located. Most often they will suggest it be built close to current lodging inventory.
2. Downtown–Many cities over the past several decades have seen their city centers go into a state of decline. City planners look for synergy centers to help revitalize a city core. One way to get large numbers of people back downtown is to build a center there. Helping to rebuild a city core has influenced a number of center location decisions.

3. In an area to be revitalized–A number of cities–New York and Washington, for example–have located new centers in areas they hope to revitalize. Locating a new center in a "run-down" part of town is an excellent way to re-energize an area. Once a center is built, it often serves as the major stimulus for the building of new hotels, restaurants, rental car agencies, and so forth in the area.

4. To save an old building or take advantage of one–Athens, Georgia, built a new center around a historic fire station. The original building has been converted to a very unique meeting space. Madison, Wisconsin, incorporated an existing Frank Lloyd Wright design when building a center there.

5. Free land–Free is hard to beat! In a number of cases, cities have built a center where land was provided. Hotel developers have been known to provide free land to insure a center was built close to one of their properties.

6. Mike Carrier, president and CEO of the Knoxville Convention Visitors Bureau, suggests hiring a professional organization like the Urban Land Institute to assist in choosing a convention center site (personal communication, May 13, 2002).

Who will market the building?

Whoever markets the building needs to get started early. It is important to remember that most larger groups book years in advance. A full marketing team needs to be on board long before a building opens. Hiring a marketing team about the time a building opens will almost ensure terrible business for the first few years a building is operational.

There is quite often a turf battle over who will market a center. A convention and visitors bureau is usually already in existence, and they will feel that they should market the center as it markets the rest of the city. Further, since a bureau pulls together bids for major conventions/tradeshows, they will feel it will be necessary for them to market the building to ensure community success.

Center managers, on the other hand, often feel that marketing the building should be under their control. Often, building managers are held accountable for the success or failure of a building. If they are held accountable, they feel it only fair that they control the marketing process.

In North America, PricewaterhouseCoopers (2001) reports the following breakdown of how centers are marketed:

- (Centers) Responsible for all Marketing: 30%.
- (Centers) Responsible for marketing for short-term events: 52%.
- (Centers) Responsible for marketing to specific event types: 19%.

Largely, convention and visitors bureaus control the rest of the marketing process. There are three scenarios implied here:

- Convention centers control marketing.
- Convention and visitors bureaus control marketing.
- Some combined effort.

An example of a combined effort is one where CVBs control booking conventions and the center controls booking tradeshows and local events.

VII. Who will manage the building?

This is really a two-part question. The first part: Who will actually manage the building? The second part: Who will the building management report to? Before we delve into these questions, it is important to note that the overall concerns at this point are "revenue concerns." Success for management, be it public or private, will hinge on factors that are controlled by management. Some of these factors (Ross, 1999) include:

- Rental policies and rate schedules.
- Event scheduling, date protection, and booking policies (see Question VIII).
- Concession and event/building service contracts.
- On-Site parking supply and fees.
- Tenant lease terms.
- Staffing and training issues.
- Maintenance standards and expenditures.
- Energy use and conservation measures.

Who will actually manage the building?

The question at this point is whether to hire a private firm to manage the building (private management) or for government to hire their own management (public management). There are advantages to each style.

Public management allows buildings to take more of an economic impact perspective. There are some events that are more profitable to the building than to the community. Public management, not as driven by profit as private management, is thought to be in a better position to make the better community decision as opposed to simply a building decision (Ross, 1999). Since their goal is often economic impact as opposed to yearly or quarterly center profitability, public management is thought to be able to have more of a long-term view.

Private management offers some advantages as well (Ross, 1999). It should be noted that private management firms like SMG have made big inroads into center management. They have managed many centers like the Miami Beach Convention Center, the Moscone Center in San Francisco, and the Hawaii Convention Center.

Private management allows cities access to professional management. Management firms are in a position to know who the good managers are, to hire them, and to train them. Further, private management gives control of hiring to organizations interested in profit and not political patronage. In essence, private management takes the politics out of hiring and booking policies.

Who does building management, public or private, report to?

There are a variety of models here:

- In some cities, building management reports to an office in city/county government.
- A number of cities have formed authorities for building management to report to (Smith, 1998).
- Some cities have the building management reporting to the convention and visitors bureau.
- A number of cities are merging their CVBs and their convention centers (San Diego (Wallace, 1997), Toledo, Ohio, and St. Louis (Garrett, 1994)).
- A few cities have actually formed corporations who operate the center.
- In Durham, North Carolina, the county and city built the Durham Civic Center but, according to a local official, "sold the air rights atop the building to a hotel developer on condition that the hotel operate the public portion."

What will be the center's booking policies?

There is often a conflict here between the lodging community and center management. The lodging community wants events booked that need large numbers of hotel rooms. They will argue, in most cases correctly, that these events have the largest economic impact on a community.

Building management, on the other hand, wants to book events that are the most profitable for the building. Some of these events simply do not require many hotels rooms or have that large an economic impact on the local community. A consumer show that attracts 50 or 60 thousand local people might yield great results for the building; that is, getting a percentage of the gate, parking concessions, food and beverage concessions, and the like. However, this show might yield little in the way of impact for the whole community.

Most communities go for the economic impact model. They prefer their centers to book events that will have the biggest economic impact. This is often reflected in a center's booking policies. Most centers will only book local and consumer shows 6 to 12 months in advance so as to hold open their space for a convention or tradeshow with large sleeping room requirements. It takes a community with some sophisticated economic understanding as this often means the center will not be as profitable as it could be.

Further, there is the question of date protection. As an example, a coin show may choose to book a center. They will want some protection from another coin show booking in two weeks before their show and stealing all of their business. Many buildings will only allow one type of show or event per year or within so many months of a similar show.

We have only touched on booking policies here. Suffice it to say there are a number of factors that must be taken into account (attrition, payment, and so on).

Who will provide services in the building?

A number of services will need to be provided in the center. Convention centers are often built with multiple accesses to water, gas, electricity, phone/computer lines, and so forth because exhibitors often need these elements in their booths. Food will have to be provided somehow, as will security, cleaning, audio-visual services, and others. It is interesting to note that even in publicly managed buildings, many of these services are provided by third-party firms. In the case of the Georgia World Congress Center, 25% to 40% of these services are provided in such a way (Ross, 1999).

Food provides some insight into this service question. Centers, over the years, have provided food in a variety of ways:

1. Hire a chef and food staff and make food a profit center. This provides consistent food quality and a profit source for the building. Often, the biggest ballroom in town is at the center, and a good F&B team can make the overall product stronger. There are some questions that may emerge if a center decides to head in this direction:

   - Is food and beverage a business for government to be in?
   - Does this create publicly funded competition for private firms?

2. Designated caterer–If the food in a center is bad, it does not take long for word to get around and hurt bookings. A frustration here is for centers

that do not provide their own F&B. One way to tighten up this area is for a center to hire one designated caterer for the building. It will require an open and fair decision process or problems can emerge.

3. Designated list of caterers–Here the center allows a group of caterers who have agreed to a list of center requirements to serve food in the building. This is much more popular with local F&B providers as it gives them the chance to earn money by providing access to business in the center. Some planners prefer this also as it gives them a wider range of services to choose from and at a wider range of prices. For the center, food consistency may become a problem as does monitoring clean-up of center facilities. It should be noted that in both case 2 and 3, many centers require a 10% rebate from the caterers. This tends to drive up the cost of F&B for planners.

For an idea about other services, an article in *Convene,* "the magazine of the Professional Convention Management Association" (Ducate, 1999) provided these figures from a survey of centers on the use of "exclusive in-house services" over a two-year period:

Services	1999	1998
Food Service	86%	85%
Electrical	75%	73%
Plumbing	53%	52%
Telephone	49%	47%
Security	44%	43%
Cleaning	43%	35%
Audio-Visual	17%	16%
General Services Contractor	6%	7%

Reprinted with permission.

What design elements should be included in a center?

The easy answer to the question is . . . It depends. It depends on the mission or missions of the building. According to a study by the Center for Exhibition Industry Research (CEIR) (Sowder & Mann, 1995), a convention center must serve the needs of three groups of people:

- The visitor/attendee.
- Event managers and exhibitors or performers.
- Facilities operations management.

A number of trends seem to be emerging in this area, like high technology (Enoch & Koss, 2001), higher quality design elements as a competitive edge

(Kirkwood, 2001), and buildings designed for multi-purposes (Greusel, 2001; Skolnik, 1995). Multi-purpose building design is especially important in second-tier or regional cities as this design increases the number of potential uses for a center.

Some primary use categories for a center (Sowder & Mann, 1995), include:

- Conventions and congresses (with or without tradeshows).
- Tradeshows (public and private).
- Seminars, technical and religious conferences.
- Banquets and receptions.
- Consumer shows.
- Major community events.

The ratio of meeting space to exhibit space has been evolving ("Convention Center Roundtable," 2000). Over the past 10 years the ratio of meeting space to exhibit space has gone from 4 to 1, to 3 to 1.

This all implies the consideration of including in the design of a center:

- Tradeshow halls.
- Ballrooms.
- Break-out rooms.
- Theaters.
- Pre-function space.
- Registration areas.
- Daycare centers.
- Parking.
- Computer rooms.
- Kitchens.
- Truck bays.
- Truck staging areas.
- Areas for sporting events.
- Others.

OTHER POSSIBLE QUESTIONS

A number of professionals have reviewed this 10-point paradigm and have suggested a number of other possible points. These include, with comments, the following:

- Who will do the feasibility study? This is a good point, but usually a community is well down the decision path before a firm is hired to do such a study. Often, at this point, a community is much more interested in how big to build a center and what design elements to include in the building rather than whether or not to build a center (Blosser, 1996). An excellent example of a request for proposal (RFP) for a convention center feasibility study has been put together by David Heinl who heads the Greater Raleigh Convention and Visitors Bureau.

Richard Chambless, owner and president of Host South in Savannah, and others have expressed the opinion that a community has largely made up its mind to build a center by the time they consider financing a feasibility study. The expense of feasibility studies are often so large that a community has to be rather sure of the outcome to initiate one in the first place. David Heinl, on the other hand, has indicated that such studies go a long way toward "lending credibility" to the idea of building a center for a broader community audience.

- Who will design and build the center (Blosser, 1996)? The American Institute of Architects have a web site that lists people and firms who have a background in designing centers. Once designed, any number of firms are capable of simply building the structure.
- A number of people who reviewed this paper (Reyn Bowman and others) felt that a community really needs to begin a convention center feasibility process with a complete inventory of the community's visitor product. This could then be followed by an analysis of whether or not a given community could be competitive in the meetings market.

CLOSING THOUGHTS

There is no way to include every possible point a community must consider when exploring the possibility of building a convention center. The intent of this paper was to outline major points communities have had to consider in the past to provide insight for communities in future planning situations.

It should be noted that the building of convention centers is probably in the mature stage of the life cycle. Any number of articles have been written that point out the large number of centers either being built or expanded (Collins, 2001; Flynn & Flynn, 1998; Merrill Lynch, 2001).

This does not mean that cities without centers should not build them. The market for center space has increased also. It does mean that future centers will have to be very specific in their mission(s). Further, future centers will need to be designed with great flexibility (Brubaker, 1998) (and high tech) in mind (Enoch & Koss, 2001; "Follow-Up: Convention Center Technology," 1999). We live in a world of high tech, but we still want high touch.

REFERENCES

Blosser, J. (1996, May/June). Facility expansion–A guide to success. *Facility Manager, XII*(3). Retrieved February 6, 2002, from www.iaam.org/articles/IAAMArticles. dll/Show?ID=742

Brubaker, S. (1998, November/December). Turn of the century convention centers. *Facility Manager, XIV*(6). Retrieved April 2002 from http://www/iaam.org/articles/ IAAMArticles.dll/Show?ID=823

Collins, M. (2001, June). Conference centers: Meetings by design. *Meeting Professional, 21*(6) Retrieved April 2002 from http//www.mpiweb.org/news/tmp/2001/ 06/conf.htm

Convention center roundtable. (2000, October). *Convene.* Retrieved April 2002 from http://www.pcma.org/resources/convene/ar-chives/displayArticle.asp?ARTICLE_ID=3862

Convention Income Survey Report. (2000). Washington, D.C.: The International Association of Convention and Visitor Bureaus Foundation.

Conventions in the U.S. & Las Vegas "101." (2001, July 3). New York: Merrill Lynch.

Dobrian, J. (2000, July). The right space for the right space: Convention center development. *Meeting Professional, 20*(7). Retrieved February 5, 2002, from www. mpiweb.org/news/tmp/acrhive.asp

Ducate, D. (1999, October). Convention centers: Ten reasons why exhibitions will be a growth industry in the next millennium. *Convene,* 5.

Enoch, M., & Koss S. (2001, November/December). Technology takes center stage in future facilities. *Facility Manager.* Retrieved May 2002 from http://www.iaam.org/ Facility_manager/Pages/2001_Nov-dec?Feature_5.htm

Flynn, M., & Flynn, L. K. (1998, March). Facility boom. *EXPO Magazine.* Retrieved February 7, 2002, from http://www.expoweb.com/expomag/BackIssues/1998/ 0398_facilityboom.htm

Follow-up: Convention center technology. (1999, February). *Convene,* 41.

Garrett, C. (1994, January/February). The conventional method. *Facility Manager, 10*(1). Retrieved May 2002 from http://www.iaam.org/articles/IAAMArticles.dll/ Show?ID=7

Greusel, D. (2001, May/June). Combination platters: Smaller convention centers serve up multiple venues to stay competitive. *Facility Manager.* Retrieved April 2002 from http://www.iaam.org/Facility_manager/Pages/2001_May_Jun/Feature_3b. htm

Kirkwood, H. (2001, February). Built to serve: Convention centers old and new keep up with the times. *EXPO Magazine.* Retrieved April 2002 from http://www. expoweb.com/expomag/BackIssues/2001/Feb/feature3.htm

Mann, N. (2000, October). It takes a community: Boston's 10-year battle to build a new convention center. *Convene.* Retrieved May 2002 from http://www.pcma.org/ ConveneScripts/Convene.dll/Show?ID=1713

PricewaterhouseCoopers. *1999 convention & congress center annual report.* Tampa, FL: PricewaterhouseCoopers.

PricewaterhouseCoopers. *2000 convention & congress center annual report.* Tampa, FL: PricewaterhouseCoopers.

PricewaterhouseCoopers. *2001 convention & congress center annual report.* Tampa, Florida: PricewaterhouseCoopers.

Ross, J. R. (1999, October). Who is minding the store? The case for public management [Electronic version]. *Convene,* 42.

Rutherford, D. G. (1990). *Introduction to the conventions, expositions and meeting industry.* New York:Van Nostrand Reinhold.

Skolnik, R. (1995, May). Multipurpose facilities. *EXPO Magazine.* Retrieved April 2002 from http:/www.expoweb.com/expomag/BackIssuues/1995/0595_mpfs.htm

Smith, T. (1998, March/April). CVB mergers: Becoming a "merchant of change." *Facility Manager, XIV*(2). Retrieved April 2002 from http://www.iaam.org/articles/IAAMArticles.dll/Show?ID=793

Sowder, R. R., & Mann, D. (1995, July). *Convention center planning: An examination of the critical issues.* Bethesda, MD: Center for Exhibition Industry Research.

Vasos, D. (2000, January). Industry profile: An *EXPO* special report. *EXPO Magazine,* 51-55.

Wallace, C. (1997, September/October). A winning team: San Diego Convention Center & CVB. *Facility Manager, XIII*(5). Retrieved April 2002 from http://www.iaam.org/articles/IAAMARticles.dll/Shwo?ID=765

So You Want to Build a Convention Center: The Case of Hope versus Reality

Richard G. McNeill, EdD
Ronald A. Evans, BS

SUMMARY. This is a case study of a convention center development project in the university town of Flagstaff, Arizona. The case answers the question: What can a project management team planning a complex public/private/public convention center project realistically expect in the first phase of the project? Hope is presented as city leaders' probable initial preparation using linear planning through the Project Management Process Model. Reality is presented as Phase I of the model unfolds and intended plans quickly diverge from expectations. The Hope/Reality Gap offers lessons-learned. *[Article copies available for a fee from The Haworth Document Delivery Service: 1-800-HAWORTH. E-mail address: <docdelivery@haworthpress.com> Website: <http://www.HaworthPress.com> © 2004 by The Haworth Press, Inc. All rights reserved.]*

KEYWORDS. Intended plan, emergent plan, convention center development, project management process model, project planning process groups

Richard G. McNeill is Associate Professor, School of Hotel and Restaurant Management, Northern Arizona University, Flagstaff, AZ.

Ronald A. Evans is Dean, School of Hotel and Restaurant Management, Northern Arizona University, Flagstaff, AZ.

Address correspondence to: Richard G. McNeill, P.O. Box 5638, Flagstaff, AZ 86011 (E-mail: Richard.McNeill@nau.edu).

[Haworth co-indexing entry note]: "So You Want to Build a Convention Center: The Case of Hope versus Reality." McNeill, Richard G., and Ronald A. Evans. Co-published simultaneously in *Journal of Convention & Event Tourism* (The Haworth Hospitality Press, an imprint of The Haworth Press, Inc.) Vol. 6, No. 1/2, 2004, pp. 23-43; and: *Current Issues in Convention and Exhibition Facility Development* (ed: Robert R. Nelson) The Haworth Hospitality Press, an imprint of The Haworth Press, Inc., 2004, pp. 23-43. Single or multiple copies of this article are available for a fee from The Haworth Document Delivery Service [1-800-HAWORTH, 9:00 a.m. - 5:00 p.m. (EST). E-mail address: docdelivery@haworthpress.com].

http://www.haworthpress.com/web/JCET
© 2004 by The Haworth Press, Inc. All rights reserved.
Digital Object Identifier: 10.1300/J452v06n01_03

INTRODUCTION

Over the last 30 years, meetings and conventions growth in the United States has been nothing less than spectacular. Understandably, cities, small, medium and large, have been engaged in a metaphorical gold rush seeking a piece of the action. The glitter of this "economic development gold" has mesmerized many city fathers throughout the last several decades and continues today. Their rallying cry seems to be a resounding, "Let's build a convention center in our town and they will come." Emblematic of this mad rush, David Ghitelman (1995), in *Meetings and Conventions Magazine*, wryly observed:

> They started out inconspicuously enough, in the downtowns of the nation's principal cities. Slowly, they got bigger. They spread to smaller cities and such emergent pleasure domes as Las Vegas and Orlando. Now, they're everywhere–big city, small city, suburb. And they keep getting bigger. Can no one stop them? Like bug-eyed aliens in a '50s horror flick, convention centers seem to have taken on a life of their own. (p. 48)

Often, it appears, the light of *reality* has been eclipsed by euphoric *hopes*. The otherwise measured and sober circumspection by city leaders seems to have been swept aside by a tidal wave of gold-rush fever.

Heywood T. Sanders, a professor of pubic administration and chair of the Public Administration Department at the University of Texas, cautioned second-tier cities just trying to enter the convention derby. He says that civic leaders looking to revitalize downtown business districts are increasingly turning to convention centers as a quick fix, regardless of whether the site makes sense or even if the city has what it takes to become a bona fide meetings destination (Sanders, 2002, August).

David Ghitelman had observed this quick-fix and me-too tendency seven years earlier:

> The tendency is for leaders to imitate the development strategies of other cities. For some cities, convention centers can work. The center can take advantage of a whole set of public amenities. The problem arises when cities that have fewer amenities and are less well-located think they can succeed with the same strategy. (Ghitelman, 1995, p. 55)

One can easily understand city fathers' succumbing to the lure of increased tourism dollars. After all, tourism is a relatively clean industry, a source of jobs, and holds the hope of a rising tax base. Revenue from meetings and conventions is perceived as a cache of gold nuggets openly exposed in the stream and just waiting to be picked up.

At approximately $2.5 billion in the early 1970s, meetings and conventions revenue has mushroomed to an estimated $115 billion in direct spending today. As a result of the *multiplier effect* applied to this direct spending, demand for auxiliary goods and services also rose. The estimated total effect from the meetings and convention business in the United States is $315.4 billion supporting 3.84 million full-time equivalent jobs (Astroff & Abbey, 2002).

Albeit periodically and temporarily slowed by cyclical recessions, even after decades of booming times, the gold rush has continued. Over the last 30 years, cities of every size have readily embarked on this journey. However, the easy gold claims have increasingly become mined out and the late-comers to the gold streams have begun to discover that the path to riches is a narrow, winding, and sometimes torturous journey. This difficult journey may be further exacerbated into the foreseeable future from the economic fallout of 9/11 and the United States' actions/counteractions against Iraq and other global threats.

In August 2002, Heywood Sanders published an extensive study, "Convention Myths and Markets: A Critical Review of Convention Center Feasibility Studies," in the scholarly *Economic Development Quarterly*. His findings were as follows:

> American cities are seeing a boom in the development of convention centers. In city after city, massive public investment in convention facilities has been justified by feasibility and market studies that consistently portray a booming national demand for exhibition space. These studies also suggest that the demand for convention center space has and will outrun increases in the supply of space. Studies for more than 30 cities demonstrate that they have been consistently flawed and misleading. Some analyses argue that successful convention centers need to expand to remain competitive. Others conclude that failing centers need to add space to succeed. Studies repeat the same positive findings verbatim from one city to another and fail to account for contradictory data. These market and feasibility studies thus offer no real basis for public investment and serve to bias public decision making and choice. (p. 195)

In a December 2000 *Wall Street Journal* article, Robert Hazard, Strategic Advisory Board Inc. (Atlanta, Georgia) partner, advised that not all cities should take the risk of chasing the lure of convention center development. Certainly cities around the United States are building convention centers in an effort to attract trade shows and conventions; however, there is significant risk. He further elaborated that most city-owned convention centers are paid for through bond issues and then repaid from hotel and automobile rental taxes. Sometimes, however, extra funding comes from a city's general revenues. Economic risk, Hazard observed, is inherent in these ventures and cities should be alert to these risks as well as the lure of rewards ("Small Cities," 2000).

John Jesitus, in his article "Cities, Developers Review Roles" (1997), reported the then current perspectives of seasoned convention center experts. These experts conveyed their experienced wisdom to representatives of many U.S. cities. In May 1997, hotel development and investment experts met in Denver with city representatives to discuss the impact of hotel/convention center development. Cities from throughout the region gathered at "A Town Meeting on Public-Private Hotel Development" to examine the impact such development would have on large and small communities alike. The Colorado Community Revitalization Association, HVS International, and the University of Colorado at Denver's Graduate School of Public Affairs hosted the event. Greg Hartmann, managing director of HVS's Denver office and moderator of the event, commented (as cited in Jesitus, 1997):

> With a growing number of municipalities offering subsidies and other development help, cities must understand the hotel industry in terms of segmentation, consolidation, and other forces. In the past, I've been hired as a consultant to work for the city or the developer or whomever, and it seems as if they're all coming from completely different perspectives. (p. 1)

At the Colorado conference, one attorney commented on a prevalent public/private convention center venture deal-killer: "[Know your politics]. If you're isolated or fighting someone else's vision, your project is doomed from the beginning."

"Watch your step," cautioned Richard Krieg in his 1996 article "Warding Off the Convention Center Blues" (1996, p. 14). He reported that since convention centers deliver over $100 billion in direct economic impact a year, it's not surprising that local governments continue to set their sights on newer and larger facilities. Increasingly, however, communities are discovering that trade shows are not as lucrative as they once thought. Few new shows are being created, and the competition to capture them has become fierce. Further, Krieg observed,

> As a result of these and other trends, convention center development can be a risky business—*one that cities often don't adequately plan for* [italics added]. Decisions to build new facilities are often based on a cursory review of national markets and a loose assessment of a city's ability to meet the needs of business travelers. (1996, p. 15)

In summary, observers of recent trends of the meeting and convention industry seem to be offering thematic advice: Convention development is a risky business and many cities should think and plan realistically before rushing forward. The siren song of "economic development gold" is compelling, but the song can deafen *reality* with *hope*.

So how can city fathers traveling the path of convention center development best prepare themselves for this perilous journey? How can the tendency for emotional hopes be balanced with probable realities? The answer to these questions is the primary purpose of this article.

We have assumed a simple logic to the foregoing discussion: hopeful expectations often conflict with the complexities of reality. To support this argument, we first acknowledge commonly expected and hopeful planning approaches and then, in the case study, show how emergent realities create a gap between the expected and the experienced. We conclude with lessons learned. The article is organized as follows.

First, the traveler's normal preparations for the metaphorical gold-rush journey will be acknowledged. This will provide a comparative starting point for a case study that is later presented. Travelers embarking on the journey to attain economic development gold may recognize many of their own assumptions and expectations about their planned journey. At this point, they would normally obtain a map. So we present a linear Project Management Process Model (Figure 1), acknowledging that planners normally begin such journeys with a definitive plan. Then the travelers would then need to know how to read a map. Here we will acknowledge project planners' intuitive knowledge that the best laid plans are usually disrupted. However, we present research that not only confirms this intuition, but provides more perspective. A view of strategy and planning will be presented to give the travelers a sense of balance between Intended Plans (Hopes) and Emergent Plans (Reality).

Second, the travelers will come face-to-face with the realities of the gold-rush journey. In the case study later described, the travelers will hear stories and be given lessons learned by an experienced traveler who has made this journey in the past. These lessons will help the travelers move past "detours," "washed out bridges," and "false turns," so to speak.

The pre-printed map that has been provided is only a starting point. The experiences of the case study vividly point out pitfalls that can easily destroy initial expectations. This is especially true when embarking on complex public/private convention center development projects.

Comparing the travelers' hopeful starting point with the realities of the case study will provide a useful primary lesson: hopeful initial plans and expectations are often dashed on the rocks of dynamic forces of emergent reality. We hope that this major lesson and the many secondary lessons presented in the

FIGURE 1. The Project Management Process Model

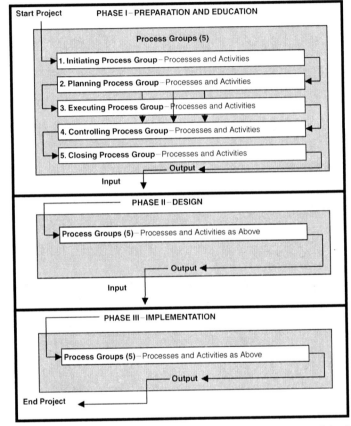

Source: Adapted from Project Management Institute, *A Guide to the Project Management Body of Knowledge (PMBOK®Guide) 2000 Edition.* Project Management Institute, Inc. 2000.

conclusion of this article will help future travelers negotiate the perilous road to successfully developing a convention center.

ACKNOWLEDGING COMMON PREPARATIONS FOR THE JOURNEY– HOPES

The Map. Travelers need to prepare for most journeys by obtaining a map. This map provides the hope of a smooth path to be followed to reach the journey's destination. In preparing for embarking on a project management venture, it is likely that planners would require some type of map. One that offers hopes of a direct journey is a classic and almost textbook map for project development as the one represented by the Project Management Process Model (Figure 1). This model not only acknowledges the expected path to project management that might be taken, but also helps to organize the reporting of the events in the case study described in this article.

The development of a convention center fits the definition of a project: "A project is a temporary endeavor undertaken to create a unique product or service" (Duncan, 1996, p. 4). The following case study began the convention center development journey with a map. The Project Management Process Model illustrated in Figure 1 provided an initial map to begin the process of preparation, design, and implementation of the convention center. It also provided common terminology and milestones for all people involved in this project. However, as will be demonstrated in the case study, detours and roadblocks occurred early in Phase I and the project became stuck in this phase for 6 years. As an initial Intended Plan, the various steps of the model serve as reference points indicating where the plan diverged from intended and became emergent. We will see these divergent points in the conclusion of this article, "Lessons Learned."

Let's briefly examine the basic components of the Project Management Process Model (Figure 1).

Phase I. Preparation/Education is concerned with the convention center project management team's basic understanding of the nature of the convention development task. Here the project team is provided basic tools and provisions to take a journey in search of "economic development gold." This phase is the most important step since it solidifies the concept of the project and develops the project's infrastructure. Phase II and III should flow smoothly once Phase I is firmly in place. (Note: The case study in this article only covers Phase I.)

Phase II. Design is concerned with the fulfillment of preparation work completed in Phase I.

Phase III. Implementation is the realization of the Design Phase.

Each phase contains five essential groups of processes named Process Groups: (a) Initiating Processes, (b) Planning Processes, (c) Executing Processes, (d) Controlling Processes, and (e) Closing Processes.

Each of the three phases repeats the same five process groups with their unique generic activity statements. It is useful to think of the Project Management Process Model as a linear input/output model where Phase I is the input to Phase II which inputs to Phase III. It is also instructive to think of each of the five process groups as a self-contained mini-project that also operates as an input/output system where the activities are interrelated. Note the reciprocating arrows within the Project Management Process Model (Figure 1) that indicate that the input/output process flow is not always linear (McNeill, 2001).

Baker and Baker (1998) provide an explanation of activities found in each of these five process groups and which vary in treatment depending on the phase under discussion:

Initiating Process Group–recognizes that a project or next phase/process should begin and commits to do so. This process stresses the formation of a project team, development of a vision for a project, and establishment of goals. Some common group process activities are:

1. Recognizing that a project should be done.
2. Determining what the project should accomplish.
3. Defining the overall project goal.
4. Defining general expectations of customers.
5. Defining the general project scope.
6. Selecting initial members of the project team.

Planning Process Group–devising and maintaining a workable scheme to accomplish the business need that the project was undertaken to address. This process defines resources required to complete the project, creates timelines, and establishes a budget. Here, objectives for various stakeholders and project team members are established. Some common group process activities are:

1. Refining the project scope, which includes identifying the balance required among results, time, and resources.
2. Listing tasks and activities that will lead to achieving the project goals.
3. Sequencing activities in the most efficient manner possible.
4. Developing a workable schedule and budget for assigning resources to the activities required to complete the project.
5. Getting the plan approved by the appropriate stakeholders.

Executing Process Group–coordinating people and other resources to carry out the plan. These processes involve coordinating and guiding the project team members to get work done as laid out and approved. It stresses keeping resources and people focused on the work. Some common group process activities are:

1. Leading the team.
2. Meeting with team members.
3. Communicating with stakeholders.
4. Firefighting (conflict resolution) to resolve problems that always arise during a project.

5. Securing necessary resources (money, people, equipment, time) to carry out the project plan.

Controlling Process Group–ensuring that project objectives are met by monitoring and measuring progress and taking corrective action when necessary. These processes are about monitoring the project. Deviations from plan need to be dealt with so that they do not adversely affect the end results of the project. Here the stress is on understanding unexpected delays, cost overruns, or changes in scope. Some common group process activities are:

1. Monitoring deviation from the plan.
2. Taking corrective action to coordinate the actual progress with the plan.
3. Receiving and evaluating project changes requested from stakeholders and team members.
4. Rescheduling the project as necessary.
5. Adapting resource levels as necessary.
6. Changing (usually cutting) the project scope.
7. Returning to the planning stage to make adjustments to the project goals and getting them approved by the stakeholders.

Closing Process Group–bringing the project or phase to an orderly end. If the closing process is part of an intermediate phase, these closing processes stress maintaining momentum to carry commitment into subsequent phases. If the closing process is the final phase of the entire project, these closing processes stress reporting and gaining acceptance of the end product. Some common group process activities are:

1. Acknowledging achievement and results.
2. Shutting down the operations and disbanding the team.
3. Learning from the project experience.
4. Reviewing the project process and outcomes with team members and stakeholders.
5. Writing a final project report.

The Project Management Process Model is presented to acknowledge a common linear approach to planning. As will be later discussed, a linear plan or intended plan is an imperative first step in project management; however, the realistic planner must expect an emergent plan to unfold. The case study exemplifies such an emergent pattern.

How to Read the Map. An initial intentional plan offers the best hope for a successful future. It is a pre-printed map of the territory. Embracing the emergent plan that unfolds and evolves from the dynamic forces that alter this intentional initial plan describes the reality of this journey. Thus, when travelers in the present read their map, their perspective must be that pre-printed maps only *represent* the territory; they are *not* the territory.

Henry Mintzberg, Bruce Ahlstrand, and Joseph Lampel, in their 1998 book, offer us a view of the dynamic and emergent nature of strategic and project planning as compared to the static and often linear way most planners are trained. Their message is clear: hope for an expected future by designing initial intentional plans in the present, but embrace the reality of divergence from these initial intentional plans during implementation.

One common definition of *strategy* is a plan that looks forward. It is a direction, a guide, a course of action into the future, or a path to get from here to there. Another, less common, definition conceives *strategy* as a pattern that is shaped from past organizational behavior and describes the actual path followed from the past to the future. From the vantage point of being in the future and looking back at what actually happened, *strategy* is defined, in this second definition, as consistency of behavior over time.

Both of the above definitions are valid: Organizations develop plans for their future–an *intended strategy*–but organizations also evolve patterns out of their past–an *emergent strategy*. Out of the 10 separate Strategy Schools categorized by Mintzberg, Ahlstrand, and Lampel, three were Intended Strategies (looking forward to expected organizational behavior); for example, Design School, Planning School, and Positioning School. Seven were Emergent Strategies (looking backward to past patterns); for example, the Learning School, the Environmental School, and the Cultural School (1998).

The key lesson to learning how to read the map is this: expect and embrace significant change from your initial map guiding the journey, but don't mistake the map for the territory. This is especially true as the complexity of the project increases.

At this point, the travelers on the journey for "economic development gold" have been outfitted with a starting map and educated on how to read the map with a balanced perspective. Thus, with these expected *hopes* for the journey, we now turn to the case study where the travelers meet *reality*.

THE CASE STUDY

Methodology

Problem Statement. What can a project management team planning a complex public/private/public conference center project realistically expect in the first phase of the project?

(Note: The term *public/private/public* is used since this case involves two separate public entities (one at local governmental level and one at state level) and one private entity (real estate/hotel developer). Adding two separate public entities plus a private entity in a joint venture amplifies the complexity of this case; therefore, we make a distinction from the commonly used term *public/private*.)

The Model–A Guide to Reporting the Case. The Project Management Process Model (Figure 1) describes a rational flow of the phases and processes of a generic project. It is a textbook derived model and one that might be used by planners attempting to plan and implement a project. It did not develop as a result of this case, but instead is a textbook model that was used as an organizational device to report the project activities of this case. Further comparison of the idealized model and the actual activities of this case help to emphasize the challenges involved in the complex project described in this case. The reader can more readily observe gaps between the ideal and actual, and lessons learned from the case are placed in a broader perspective.

The title of this article, "So You Want to Build a Convention Center: The Case of Hope versus Reality," reflects the gap between the rational approach that this model suggests and the realities of a complex and dynamic environment. Rational managers often believe that such a project management model can be designed *a priori* and then, with will and determination, force future dynamics to comply with the model. The gaps observed between the ideal model and the actualities of the case will quickly dispel this fantasy.

Single Case–Qualitative Research. Benefits of this single case study can be found in two areas: content and process. Content lessons are found in reporting an experience from which others can reap practical lessons: "do's and taboos." Process lessons are provided since the study illustrates the first phase of a "project management" model that provides a commonly used linear planning model and set of standard procedures away from which emergent or unforeseen deviations will most likely follow.

Limitations are also found in both content and process in this case. Content limitations include the fact that this is a single case that reports the first phase of project development of a complex public/private/public convention center project in a small western university town. These specific characteristics may not be fully representative of the wide variations found in other cities and towns considering a similar project. Process weaknesses include variations between the initial foundation level of experience of this case's project sponsors and managers as compared with other projects' sponsors and managers considering developing a convention center. These variations include such things as (a) political abilities, (b) organization skills, and (c) project management experience.

Scope of the Case Study

This case does not cover all three phases of the model described in Figure 1. Due to breakdowns and obstacles, the project stalled in Phase I–Preparation and Education. It has been stalled in this initial phase for 6 years.

Source of Data

The second author of this article is within the leadership structure of the task force that is sponsoring the effort to develop a conference center in Flagstaff, Arizona. His access to all documents regarding this case and his direct involvement in this project have provided substantial and substantive data to enable accurate reporting of this case study.

Setting of the Case Study

Flagstaff is a medium-sized university town located at the crossroads of north/south I-17 and east/west I-40. These are the two most heavily traveled arterials in northern Arizona. Historic Route 66 passes through the center of town and it has traditionally served as a tourism pass-through to the Grand Canyon National Park.

Business leaders have long desired to make the community more of a destination area, and to that end began to recognize the need for convention facilities to address the growing demand for meeting space within the community and the greater region.

Currently, three out of every four jobs in the city of Flagstaff are tourism related (Morrison Institute, 2000). Many civic leaders believe that a convention center and supporting infrastructure will facilitate extended stays by group visitors, increase dollars spent in the community year-round, increase sales and bed, board, and booze (BBB) tax revenues, plus increase construction, operations, and tourism economic multipliers to the area.

At an elevation of 7,000 feet, Flagstaff is surrounded by towering mountains, large state and national parks with stands of Ponderosa pine trees and is situated as a gateway to many Native American reservations. It is the home of both pro-growth advocates and conservationists. These often opposing forces are key factors in the complexity of political decisions in Flagstaff, Arizona.

Phase I–Preparation and Education

The following account of the events that occurred in Phase I have been organized to best parallel the five process groups discussed regarding the Project

Management Process Model (Figure 1). Synchronization of events with process groups is imperfect but, hopefully, instructive.

Initiating Process Group. In February 1997, the Flagstaff Chamber of Commerce created a task force of local business, university, and political leaders to study and determine the appropriateness of a convention center complex for the city to be developed as a public/private partnership. Included in the leadership of this task force was one of the authors of this article.

After several meetings, a feasibility study was commissioned to ascertain consumer demand, size and scope of the project, and potential site locations (Economics Research Associates, 1998).

In July 1998, the findings of the feasibility study were presented to the city council with a recommended development of a 41,000 square foot convention center, a 250 room full-service hotel, a 6,000 seat multi-purpose arena, and a 1,200 seat performing arts theater.

As the task force continued its work to define the proposed project, three primary issues were discussed: (a) what facilities were desired, (b) what location and private sector partner(s) would be sought, and (c) how would the project be financed. At this point, the performing arts theater was dropped from the project for reasons of cost containment and redundancy. Existing facilities existed at Northern Arizona University (NAU) and were available to the community. It was also decided that the project be referred to as a *conference center* rather than a *convention center*. This designation clarification was due to the actual size and nature of the proposed facility as well as to the public's potentially negative perception and reception of a large project in an environmentally sensitive community.

Planning Process Group. In December 1998, the task force issued a Request for Information (RFI) to determine interest from potential private developers. In due course, seven were received for consideration.

At this point, the project planning process began to depart from the linear textbook model briefly outlined in Figure 1. Because Flagstaff is a community containing many polarized factions (such as pro-growth, anti-growth, environmentalists, pro-tourism, and anti-tourism to name a few), the task force decided it should test voter sentiment through a survey and focus groups.

In March 1999, the Social Research Laboratory at NAU conducted an omnibus Flagstaff study which contained questions about the proposed project. The results showed a 64% response in favor of a conference center, with 26% opposed to the idea and another 10% with no opinion (Social Research Lab, 1999).

Following the survey, focus groups were conducted by the Arizona Hospitality Research and Resource Center, the research arm of the School of Hotel and Restaurant Management at NAU. Once again, the results were in support of a conference center project in the community (Cothran, 1999).

In August of 1999, a progress report was given to the city council and county board of supervisors. Four primary sites were reviewed by city staff. Two public meetings were held at the city library. There was a sparse turnout for both meetings, but those attending were supportive of the project.

By December 1999, two parties were considered to have the most serious interest in developing the project–the owners of Little America hotel chain and NAU. The task force floated the idea of a .5% increase in the BBB tax to be put to the voters at the next election and that the increase, if passed, be earmarked to help pay for the conference center. Also at this time, a casino developer met with the task force and wanted their support in building a conference center complex plus a casino on Indian lands about 10 miles outside of the city. Task force opinions were split on this concept, and they wanted time to consider the pros and cons of the idea. Regardless of one's opinion on casino gaming, this request at this time provided another divergence from the critical path in the project planning process.

In January 2000, the task force retained a Phoenix consultant who recommended that additional information was needed before going to the public for a vote on a proposed BBB tax increase. Specifically, the consultant observed three important information gaps. First, there was no shared project vision among the leadership in the community to present to the voters. Second, an impact study was needed to inform the voters of the positive economic advantages for the community. Third, a legal opinion from the city was needed regarding the use of public funds being used to support assets on private land and state university land.

The added challenge of needing to gain funding support from the voters at the ballot box created a further widening of the gap between the guiding rational planning process model and the realities of trying to structure a public/private project. The task force responded by ordering an impact study and continuing to work on clarifying the project components to present to the city council.

In April 2000, the impact study was completed, and it added another positive argument for developing the project (Pollack, 2000). After considering the casino gaming proposal and weighing its probable support by the voters, the task force decided to drop this option from future consideration. They also decided not to pursue increasing the BBB tax at the next election as there were too many competing public works tax bills already on the ballot.

Executing Process Group. In August 2000, city/chamber representatives met with Little America executives to discuss potential financial incentive options available to them and determine their interest in developing the project on their site. They then met with NAU representatives to determine their interest in developing the project on university land. Both parties expressed continued interest, and in February 2001, the task force decided to issue a non-binding Request for Proposal (RFP) for the project development (Request for Proposal, 2001a).

With the community sending a strong signal through the chamber of commerce that it wanted to move forward, NAU decided it should take steps to formalize its interest. These steps served to widen the gap even further between the original linear planning process and the actual evolving process by adding another potential partnership entity. At this point, the situation had evolved into exploring a partnership structure that included the city, the private sector, and a public university. The former prosaic public/private partnership had expanded into a complex public/private/public partnership.

In May 2001, NAU determined that the only way they could be a participant was by providing a ground lease to a private developer who would build a conference center complex that served both the city and NAU's needs. Any proposed structure would also have to insulate the university from any contingent financial liability to the project. This added an additional timeline and complexity to the planning process as the required development steps that must be taken at a public university were now layered on to the ever-expanding planning process.

Controlling Process Group. On June 4, 2001, NAU issued a Request for Offers (RFO) on a ground lease for the expressed purpose of creating a conference center complex consisting of a conference center, hotel, arena, residence life facility, and a new building for the School of Hotel and Restaurant Management (Request for Offers, 2001).

NAU received one solid response and upon evaluation it was determined that the financial aspects of the offer were very promising. The offer would also meet the institutional goal of enhancing NAU's School of Hotel and Restaurant Management by furnishing significant new laboratory facilities for its students (School of Hotel and Restaurant Management, 2001). Additionally, this would fulfill the shared community goal of creating a conference center and arena which would provide an entertainment venue currently unavailable in northern Arizona.

On June 28, 2001, NAU informed the Arizona Board of Regents that it wished to respond to the chamber's RFP with a tentative proposal based on the RFO response that the university had received for the development of a conference center complex. The Arizona Board of Regents denied NAU's request as presented, but authorized NAU to submit an expanded RFP to a broader spectrum of qualified firms or individuals over an eight-week period with a proposal due date of September 18, 2001.

An RFP was issued (Request for Proposal, 2001b). Eight companies showed interest and four submitted formal responses. Unfortunately, all of the responses fell short of protecting the university from financial contingent liabilities in the event of operational shortfalls, so NAU officially withdrew the RFP in order to assess financial implications to the university and to commission a market study to derive a current financial pro-forma for the project (Northern Arizona University, 2002). At the beginning of 2002, both NAU and Little America were still interested in the project, but neither was prepared to respond to the task force's request for proposal.

The task force continued work with city officials and other interested parties throughout most of 2002, which culminated in the city of Flagstaff officially issuing its own RFP on September 15, 2002, for a 20,000 square foot conference center, a 250-room four-to five-star hotel, a parking garage, and an associated retail complex. The city's preferred location was in the historic downtown area in the Downtown Redevelopment District, but the city was willing to consider other locations that would provide similar benefits to the community (Request for Proposal, 2002). Proposals were due on March 14, 2003, 6 years after the initial meeting of the chamber's convention center task force which began the process.

As of this writing and after a difficult six-year life of Phase I of the Flagstaff, Arizona, convention center development project, this Phase I of the conference center project has not yet been closed. The difficulties continue today and are likely to persist into the foreseeable future.

As reported in early March 2003 by Jeff Tucker in the local Flagstaff, Arizona paper, *Arizona Daily Sun*, the last RFP issued by the city (Request for Proposal, 2002) was answered by six private hotel/real estate developers (Tucker, 2003). Additionally, Tucker reported that the Flagstaff City Redevelopment Coordinator, Michael Kerski, "hopes to have a tentative agreement in place by June or July [2003]" (Tucker, 2003, p. D1).

Further, Tucker reported, "neither Northern Arizona University's School of Hotel and Restaurant Management nor Little America, both major players in this project, submitted proposals" (Tucker, 2003, p. D1).

Closing Process Group. This case initially began as a *public/private/public* venture. At this writing, one public entity (the city) is on board and six potential private entities are competing for the one *private* slot of the venture. Unfortunately, the second public entity, NAU, is not currently involved in the present RFP responses. Thus, the harmony of the original venture appears to be disrupted. Will the city downsize this project to a public/private venture by leaving out the second public, NAU? Will NAU go forward and solicit private developers and initiate its own public/private venture while leaving the city out of the game? Or will the vision of the original public/private/public venture be restored? Obviously, Phase I–Preparation and Education of the Project

Management Process Model (Figure 1) has more to be accomplished before Phase II–Design and Phase III–Implementation can begin.

CONCLUSION AND LESSONS LEARNED

Conclusion

Over the last several decades, small and medium-sized cities have been participants in an "economic development gold rush" to build convention centers. These ventures are often too readily accepted as a panacea for tourism growth without a full understanding of their true cost/benefit characteristics. Additionally, these projects are characteristically initially planned in a linear fashion as if changing future conditions could accurately be predicted during the initial planning process. Thus, intended plans evolve into emergent surprises and problems, and hopes are often painfully brought into line with realities.

The purpose of this case study was to answer the question "What can a project management team planning a complex public/private/public conference center project realistically expect in the first phase of the project?"

Metaphorically, convention center project management teams were described as travelers on a tenuous journey in search of economic development gold. To assist future travelers along the road of convention center development, this case study attempted to prepare these sojourners with the best map possible and stories from an experienced traveler.

First, we acknowledged common preparations for the journey that the project planners might take. These preparations represented their hopes for a smooth path to the destination. A map was supplied: the Project Management Process Model (Figure 1) provided an initial overview of how project management travelers normally might begin their journey. This map provided baseline direction to reach the destination–successful convention center implementation. Then the travelers were educated in how to read their map. We offered a balanced perspective regarding how intended plans and hopes are often radically altered by emergent realities.

Second and finally, we told the case study story. We related practical lessons learned by an experienced traveler who had made this journey in the past. We told how original plans (Project Management Process Model), expectations, and hopes for this project were drastically modified by the realities of the journey. Let's review the lessons learned in Phase I of the Process Management Process Model (Figure 1). We will categorize by the five process groups discussed earlier in the model.

Lessons Learned

Initiating Process Group

1. *Shared vision is mandatory.* In a politically fragmented community with many polarizing factors, it is vital that a shared vision be carefully crafted early on with a strategy to sell the vision to all stakeholders and get their buy-in.
2. *Decide what you want to accomplish.* Is the primary purpose of the convention center to boost the city's economic health or to provide public meeting space? Make that clear in your mission statement.
3. *Know your politics.* If you're isolated or fighting someone else's vision, your project is doomed from the beginning.
4. *Strong leadership is vital.* Inexperienced leadership in convention center development in a medium- to smaller-sized community tends to follow models utilized in first-tier cities. Customer demand and available infrastructure for small to medium-sized cities are very different from that found in first-tier large cities. This mistake only leads to project disillusionment.
5. *There is no free lunch!* Cities that want convention centers in their communities for economic and political reasons need to be prepared up front to go it alone with voter approved bond financing or offer specific incentives to private sector developers to strengthen the overall pro-forma of the project and reduce market risk.

Planning Process Group

1. *Review your assets and liabilities.* This means objectively appraising such factors as local and regional amenities, transportation, labor force, and municipal services. Develop a hard-nosed plan to overcome the weaknesses you uncover. The politics can get rough, so a high-powered, politically savvy group is needed to oversee this effort.
2. *Avoid euphoric hopes.* Site selection should be based on the location most favorable to the economic viability of the project, balanced with any negative impacts. Avoid the "I've got a friend that owns a nice piece of dirt that would be ideal" syndrome.
3. *Leave your cookie cutter at home.* Having the right product for the municipality is extremely important.
4. *Have a clear bid selection and negotiation process in the beginning phase of the project.* Hoteliers likewise should seek to have a community's bid selection and negotiation process up front, spelled out as clearly as possible, to prevent the possibility they'll be undercut by a local favorite at the 11th hour.

Executing Process Group

1. *Complexity invariably ensures intended plans diverge from expectations.* In multiple party ventures (public/private), more issues must be addressed, negotiated, and measured, thus such ventures are very complex. Complexity results from different visions, varying risks/returns to each partner, different processes that the public entity is required to follow that the private entity is not, and political issues that the public entity is faced with that the private entity is not. Multiple and varying venture partner's interests combine to expand the timeline of the planning process and impede expeditious project development. In this case study, a public/private/public (city/a to-be-determined private sector real estate or hotel developer/state university) venture is even more complex and difficult to drive to a successful outcome.

2. *Guard against the temptation for "project creep."* Supporting infrastructure can be critical to the overall success of the project. But how much is enough? During the planning phase of a project of large size and scope, there is a tendency to want to "add more logs on the fire." Some of these can be so politically charged that they can kill the entire project before it can get off the ground. For instance, as in this case, adding more hotel rooms in a tourism area creates political challenges, but considering an additional "log," a casino, exacerbates the challenges.

Controlling Process Group

1. *Be as open as possible with the public and press.* It's the closed meetings that can create problems for hotel developers and city council members. Keep in mind, however, that revealing too many details of a proposal too early can create needless and costly delays if local citizens are inclined to nit-pick.

2. *Control the timeline.* The longer the timeline from planning to project completion, the more difficult the project becomes. There is a greater window of risk for negatives to occur over positives–for example, economic shifts, costs of money, and political issues.

Closing Process Group

The Closing Process Group is concerned with the wrap up of the phase under consideration. It consists of the *output* that is transformed into the *input* of the next phase. Phase I must be completed before Phase II can begin. Six years after the Flagstaff Chamber of Commerce created the conference center task force in February 1997, the vision of developing a conference center remains just that: a vision stalled in the opening phase of the project.

What is the major lesson learned? It is one that not only applies to the closing process group of Phase I, but to the entire Project Management Process Model: rational hopes are often dashed on the rocks of reality. A model is a guiding map only. It is an intentional strategy or plan. It is a hope for a successful future. Be prepared for dynamic forces or reality to alter the best planned intentions.

This case study has focused on the most important phase of the Project Management Process Model: Phase I–Preparation and Education. Getting this phase right is the key to the successful flow of the remaining two phases. This case study has presented what we believe to be the most important lessons learned in this crucial phase.

So you want to build a convention center! We believe that initial *hopes* balanced with *realities* is the key to eventual success. We wish all future travelers on the journey to conference center development a successful trip and hope that stories from our recent journey will help remove many of the roadblocks, pitfalls, and detours that may be encountered.

REFERENCES

Astroff, M. T., & Abbey, J. R. (2002). *Convention sales and services* (6th ed.). Las Vegas, NV: Waterbury Press.

Baker, S., & Baker, K. (1998). *Project management.* New York: Alpha Books, Simon and Schuster Macmillan Company.

Cothran, C. (1999, June 10). *Focus groups: Flagstaff conference center.* For the conference center task force. Flagstaff, AZ: Arizona Hospitality Research and Resource Center.

Duncan, W. R. (1996). *A guide to the project management body of knowledge.* Upper Darby, PA: Project Management Institute.

Economics Research Associates. (1998, July). *Convention center feasibility and market analysis.* Prepared for the Flagstaff Chamber of Commerce Center task force by Economics Research Associates.

Ghitelman, D. (1995, February). Convention center development: Never enough. *Meetings and Conventions, 30*(2), 48-57.

Jesitus, J. (1997, April 27). Cities, developers review roles. *Hotel & Motel Management, 212*(7), 1-2.

Krieg, R. M. (1996, November). Warding off the convention center blues. *Planning, 62*(11), 4-18.

McNeill, R. G. (2001). Creating a hospitality sales management course on the web: Lessons for the beginner. *Journal of Teaching in Travel & Tourism, 1*(2/3), 125-152.

Mintzberg, H., Ahlstrand, B., & Lampel, J. (1998). *Strategy safari: A guided tour through the wilds of strategic management.* NY: Simon & Schuster, Inc.

Morrison Institute. (2000, January). *Destination Flagstaff: How important is the Flagstaff tourism cluster?* Tempe, AZ: Morrison Institute for Public Policy, Arizona State University.

Northern Arizona University. (2002, January 17). *Notice of withdrawal of RFP # PO3BG001.* Flagstaff, AZ: Northern Arizona University.

Pollack, E. D. (2000, April 12). *Economic and fiscal impact of the proposed conference center and hotel, Flagstaff, Arizona.* For the Flagstaff Chamber of Commerce.

Request for Offers. (2001, June 4). *Request for offer for lease agreement for the development of a conference center complex for Northern Arizona University.* Project # PO1BG008. RFO due date: June 18, 2001.

Request for Proposal. (2001a, February). *Request for proposal for a Flagstaff conference center.* For Flagstaff Chamber of Commerce. RFP due date: April 30, 2001.

Request for Proposal. (2001b, July 24). *Request for proposal for a lease agreement to develop a conference center complex for Northern Arizona University.* RFP # PO2BG001. RFP due date: September 18, 2001.

Request for Proposal. (2002, September 15). *Request for proposal for a hotel, conference center and parking garage for the city of Flagstaff.* RFP due date: March 14, 2003. Flagstaff, AZ: City of Flagstaff.

Sanders, H. T. (2002, August). Convention myths and markets: A critical review of convention center feasibility studies. *Economic Development Quarterly, 16*(3), 195-210.

School of Hotel and Restaurant Management. (2001, August). *A demonstration of the competitive need for program growth and facilities expansion at the School of Hotel and Restaurant Management.* Flagstaff, AZ: School of Hotel and Restaurant Management, Northern Arizona University.

Small cities build and hope tourists come. (2000, December 20). *The Wall Street Journal, CCXXXVI*(120) [Eastern, Princeton, NJ, Edition], p. B14.

Social Research Lab. (1999, March). *Omnibus survey.* Flagstaff, AZ: Social Research Laboratory at Northern Arizona University.

Tucker, J. (2003, March 2). City gets conference center bids. *Arizona Daily Sun,* p. D1.

Issues in Dedicated
Convention Center Development
with a Case Study
of the Perth Convention
and Exhibition Center,
Western Australia

Jack Carlsen, PhD

SUMMARY. Development of Dedicated Convention Centers (DCC) generates significant economic, political, and social issues for theoretical and applied studies, yet there is limited literature in this area. These issues include feasibility and funding, design and construction, and operations and marketing. To increase our understanding of the developmental and operational dimensions of these facilities, the limited literature in these areas is reviewed and a case study of the design and development of the Perth Convention and Exhibition Center (PCEC) in Western Australia is presented. The case study is chronological and describes the development of the facility from pre-feasibility stage, through design and contracting, funding and approvals to construction and pre-marketing. *[Article copies available for a fee from The Haworth Document Delivery Service: 1-800- HAWORTH. E-mail address: <docdelivery@haworthpress.com> Website: <http:// www. HaworthPress.com> © 2004 by The Haworth Press, Inc. All rights reserved.]*

Jack Carlsen is MUI Chair in Tourism and Hospitality Studies, and Co-Director, Curtin Sustainable Tourism Centre, Curtin Business School, Curtin University of Technology, Kent Street, Bentley, WA 6102, Australia (E-mail: CarlsenJ@cbs.curtin.edu.au).

[Haworth co-indexing entry note]: "Issues in Dedicated Convention Center Development with a Case Study of the Perth Convention and Exhibition Center, Western Australia." Carlsen, Jack. Co-published simultaneously in *Journal of Convention & Event Tourism* (The Haworth Hospitality Press, an imprint of The Haworth Press, Inc.) Vol. 6, No. 1/2, 2004, pp. 45-61; and: *Current Issues in Convention and Exhibition Facility Development* (ed: Robert R. Nelson) The Haworth Hospitality Press, an imprint of The Haworth Press, Inc., 2004, pp. 45-61. Single or multiple copies of this article are available for a fee from The Haworth Document Delivery Service [1-800-HAWORTH, 9:00 a.m. - 5:00 p.m. (EST). E-mail address: docdelivery@haworthpress.com].

KEYWORDS. Dedicated Convention Centers, feasibility, funding, construction, operation

INTRODUCTION

Conventions have been described as "the seams of gold that run through Australian tourism" (Sandilands, 1993, p. 3), and Dedicated Convention Centers (DCCs) could be considered the "mother lode" when it comes to realizing the economic and tourism benefits of conventions tourism. Together with meetings and exhibitions, conventions were estimated to generate AU$7 billion in direct spending in 1996/1997 in Australia, directly employ 85,000 persons, and contribute 1.5% of gross domestic product (Johnson, Foo, & O'Halloran, 1999). Western Australia (WA) attracted more than one million delegates in 1996/1997, generating AU$670 million, or 6% of total delegate expenditure in Australia. Conventions business in WA was forecast to grow at about 10% per annum from 2000 to 2004 and growth in exhibitions was forecast to be 6% per annum for the same period (Perth Convention Bureau, 2000).

The historical development of Dedicated Convention Centers (DCCs) has proven to be essential to the growth of conventions business in Australia. Adelaide was the first city to open a DCC in 1987 (Adelaide Convention Center), followed by Sydney Convention and Exhibition Center (1988), Canberra Convention Center (1989), and Melbourne Convention Center (1990). Brisbane Convention and Exhibition Center opened in 1995; a second facility in Cairns, Queensland, opened in 1996; and a third Queensland DCC on the Gold Coast is currently under construction. All of these have the high seating capacity in tiered auditoria expected in a DCC, as well as exhibition halls, breakout rooms for smaller sessions, audio-visual facilities, simultaneous translation, banqueting services, and associated tourism facilities (hotel and central business district (CBD) access). In a DCC, the capacity of the main auditorium must be at least 2,000-tiered seats, matched by at least 10 breakout rooms with audio-visual facilities for smaller meetings of up to 200 delegates.

There are also several hundred meetings venues at resorts, hotels, and casinos that have supported the growth of conventions business in Australia. Underpinning this growth in conventions business is the increased airline access and new direct services to the capital cities from major tourist generating regions. At a national level, the hosting of the Sydney 2000 Olympics and subsequent marketing efforts by the Australian Tourist Commission have also raised the profile of Australia as a conventions and events destination (McCabe, Poole, Weeks, & Leiper, 2000).

Against this background, a prolonged planning and development process commenced in WA to progress the development of a dedicated convention and exhibition center and to commence a project that had been mooted in the mid-1980s. This paper will describe the process through which the Perth Convention and Exhibition Center (PCEC) was developed and identify a range of issues that will be of interest to other cities planning to develop a DCC. Some of the key issues identified in the literature and exemplified in the case study include:

- Feasibility and funding.
- Design, location, and construction.
- Operations, management, and marketing.

LITERATURE REVIEW

There is limited academic literature specific to development of DCCs and their role in tourism destinations. Carlsen (1999) has identified infrastructure as a key area for research in the conventions and exhibitions sector, including hard (buildings) and soft (communications) infrastructure, capacity management, design and construction, and management of DCCs. Technology is now playing a major role in all aspects of conventions business, as is security and safety at conventions, particularly large, international gatherings such as the Summit on Sustainable Development in Johannesburg that attracted more than 50,000 delegates in 2002. Relevant issues that have been addressed in the literature are reviewed in the following sections.

Funding, Finance, and Feasibility Issues

In addition to the academic studies of conventions facilities, trade journals provide some insights into current issues in convention facility development. One key issue to emerge is economic and financial feasibility of convention facilities, particularly in cases where the center will be funded by public authorities. The race to develop or extend convention centers in North America in the 1980s and 1990s was driven principally by the optimistic feasibility studies and upward growth forecasts for conventions and expositions. Consequently, the number of convention centers in North America grew by 60% between 1987 and 1995, and the amount of exhibition space is expected to increase by 50% between 1998 and 2003 (Casey, 1998). The benefits to small and mid-sized cities would flow in the form of additional delegate and conference organizer expenditure on a wide range of products and services.

However, it must be recognized that not all convention cities provide the full range of services required by delegates, so economic benefits will not always "spin-off" from convention facilities. For example, airline and hotel capacity must equate with convention facility capacity if the tourism spin-off from conventions is to be fully realized. Some cities in the United States, such as Orlando and Las Vegas, have targeted conventions business knowing that they not only have world class facilities, but also the capacity, infrastructure, and amenities required by delegates. Capacity for expansion in order to accommodate the growth of existing exhibitions and conventions is also important, especially as competition for conventions business increases. Hotel development was found to follow, rather than coincide with, convention facilities in cities such as Philadelphia, Providence, and Charlotte. Cities must then urge hotel developers to honor verbal commitments that were contingent upon a center being built, according to Schuldenfrei (as cited in Casey, 1998, p. 4).

Further delays in development or expansion of convention facilities arise from the need for public funding to be approved by state or local officials and, in some cases, by the citizens through referenda. The reason that funding decisions are critical is that convention facilities generally do not recover capital costs of construction over time–they are loss leaders. The return on investment does not flow to the facilities, but instead accrues to the state economy around the center and to the tourism industry–a spin-off effect (Carlsen, 2002).

However, the global nature of conventions and exhibitions exposes the sector to adverse economic and social conditions. A number of convention centers in North America experienced declining business, due to the combined effects of recession, increased competition, and the global downturn in business travel after September 2001. Casey (1998) found that the expansion of the Lakeland convention center was in response to an anticipated 25% decline in business as exhibitors move their expanding business to larger centers. Centers in Austin, Raleigh, and other mid-sized cities face similar futures and will need to either expand or risk losing existing and new business. Turkel (2002) claims that delegate attendance for centers from New York, New York, to San Diego, California, experienced a decline in attendance since 1997, by 10% in 2000 and 7.4% in 2001. Despite this decline, Turkel claims that 36 new centers are awaiting financing and supply of facilities clearly exceeds demand. Turkel recommends the convention feasibility studies include yield-management, market penetration, and revenue maximization to avoid becoming white elephants for convention cities. Wirtz (2001) cautions that as the market size decreases, the economic arguments in favor of convention centers apply only to larger cities that have the local population that can support the center. In this scenario, the convention city citizens are effectively underwriting the operations of the center through their taxes or bond holdings, a situation that will only be alleviated when tourist flows, bed taxes, and revenue return.

Wirtz (2001) cites discrepancies in feasibility studies that are based on wrong assumptions, over-estimates of tourism flows and exaggerated economic multiplier effects in feasibility studies for sport stadia and convention centers. Other factors often overlooked in feasibility studies include "substitution effects," where local spending on conventions, exhibitions, and sports events is substituted for spending on other items in the local economy, resulting in no "new" money and no net gain for the local economy. It is only tourists from interstate and overseas that generate new money into host regions and the associated spin-off benefits for the economy. Another economic effect overlooked in feasibility studies is the opportunity cost of convention center funding, in terms of the cost of other projects (new schools and hospitals) that are foregone in order to build and operate a convention center. It could be argued that the social and economic dividends from a healthy and educated population would always exceed any returns generated by a convention center. Alternately, the "public good" values of conventions in terms of increased city pride and image, technology transfer and trade and investment that often accompany successful conventions, trade shows, and events are seldom estimated. The incidence and impact of tourist taxes and the purpose for which taxation revenue from tourism is treated as a return on investment in public infrastructure such as convention centers has not been investigated, but remains an important public issue.

Estimates of returns to convention centers are often based on estimates of delegate expenditure and attendance provided by Convention and Visitor Bureaux (CVB), who have a vested interest in "proving" the value of the conventions business in their reporting. This encourages mis-specified or overstated delegate expenditure, exaggerated multiplier effects, and large discrepancies in estimates depending on assumptions about proportions of international and interstate delegates and associated expenditure and multiplier effects. For example, Wirtz (2001) found that two estimates of economic impact of a multi-use arena in Fargo, North Dakota, ranged from U.S.$3.8 million to U.S.$15.3 million and that multipliers as high as six where used when more reliable multipliers are closer to two.

Allied to this issue of feasibility is funding. Basically there are only two sources of funding for convention centers: public or private. It could be argued that the potential negative returns on investment deter private sector investors, therefore DCCs must be publicly funded through state government building funds. This places an onus on DCCs to generate returns to the community immediately upon opening and for extended periods of time into the future. Where public-private funding arrangements are put in place, tax incentives and contractual clauses are used to entice private corporations and individuals.

For example, funding for the Osceola Convention Center was gained through the sale of U.S.$35 million in tax-exempt bonds by Osceola County (Reisman, 1999). The San Diego U.S.$100 million convention center was funded by the sale of coupon bonds maturing in 2019 and the Washington, D.C., convention center sold a U.S.$71 million tax revenue issue bearing a 5% coupon (Harris, 1999). The management contracts of centers become critical under such funding arrangements, with the center expected to generate sustained returns not only to private investors, but also to the public in general who have, after all, underwritten the facility through taxes. The legal, financial, and contractual detail of convention center funding is beyond the scope of this paper, but must be acknowledged as a critical issue in the development of DCCs.

Design, Location, and Construction Issues

Rutherford (1990) provides an overview of the design, construction, and location of convention infrastructure and the importance of meeting requirements in terms of location, appearance, and functionality of the facility. Important locational elements of a DCC include access via public and private transport from hotels, airports, and central business districts, so a central or "landmark" site is favored over remote sites that have been used in the past. External appearance is also important and DCCs have been transformed from purely functional buildings to architectural statements and tourism icons through innovative design and construction. Internally, DCCs must provide large foyer spaces for use in registration and functions, exhibition space which is column-free, and floor ratings and ceiling heights to accommodate large exhibits and structures. The requirement for column-free space has led to innovative roofing designs for DCCs, giving theses buildings a striking external appearance and extensive internal exhibition space. For example, the hyperbolic paraboloid structure of the Brisbane Convention and Exhibition Center (BCEC) allows for a clear 24,000 square meters of exhibition space and gives the external roof the appearance of sails over the Brisbane River. Similar innovations are evident in many major cities around the world, such as Vancouver, Sydney, and Hong Kong, where the roofline complements the harbor-side settings. McCabe et al. (2000) found that DCCs in the United Kingdom use a historical backdrop, such as the Houses of Parliament and Westminster Abbey in London, to project iconican status for the facility. McCabe et al. (2000) describe operational elements of DCCs in Australia and claim the Cairns convention center is Australia's first environmentally friendly convention center operation. This claim was based on the design which uses natural elements of airflow and sunlight to save energy and conserve resources during operation. In addition, the roof structure is made from plantation pine timber, not imported rainforest timbers, so that both local employment and native forest conservation is optimized during construction.

Operations, Management, and Marketing Issues

Hiller (1995) argues that large conventions are attractions in themselves, with location and setting of secondary importance, due to the delegates "commitment to the purpose of the convention" regardless of location (Hiller, 1995, p. 375). In fact, Hiller considered issues such as accessibility more important than the attractiveness of the surrounding site. The strategy of targeting conventions business as a significant tourism market has been adopted by several cities around the world seeking to achieve international recognition by hosting major international conventions. For example, Japan greatly expanded its conventions facilities in the 1990s, and the number of convention cities increased from 25 in 1992 to 46 in 1995 (Law, 1996). Japan has, to a large extent, emulated the earlier growth of convention facilities in the United States and Europe with the strategy of attracting large international meetings held by intergovernmental agencies and multinational corporations. The initial success of Japan's convention facility strategy has encouraged other Asian countries to develop DCCs and now most, if not all, boast at least one world-class convention facility. As a result, hosting large international conventions has become increasingly competitive in view of the extensive social and economic benefits that result from these "mega-conventions," and there has been some systematic research on the convention destination choice process (Oppermann, 1996) and modeling social impacts of conventions (Hiller, 1995).

The need for DCCs to produce returns on public and private investment has significant implications for the management and marketing of convention centers. It is important to recognize that the marketers of convention services in a destination are not always directly employed by DCCs and can include private marketing agencies, public destination management organizations, city convention bureaux, and federal tourism marketing agencies–the latter particularly when DCCs reach international icon status for a nation. There is also potential for cross-promotion with global hotel chains linked with the DCC, provided that the location is adjacent to hotels and tourist facilities (McCabe et al., 2000). DCC "customers" are not the end-users of the facilities (that is, the delegates). They are intermediaries that include meeting planners, professional conference organizers (PCOs), and exhibition companies. McCabe et al. (2000) refers to these as level II decision makers in the Australian convention distribution system. In destinations where the DCCs provide the only venue in the destination with the capacity and infrastructure to host the meeting, convention, or exhibition, marketing is less of an imperative. However, when competition between DCCs is intense, marketing takes on a greater level of importance, and key (level I) decision makers within associations and corporations may be targeted in marketing. Direct marketing using high quality collateral material (brochures and newsletters), familiarization tours, and personal sales pitches to decision makers are necessary. Increasingly, electronic publications and the Internet are employed to promote DCCs online and include virtual tours of the facility and a comprehensive website with all information required by meeting planners and decision makers. Having won the right to host a convention or exhibition, it is then important that the DCC partners with all other stakeholders, level I and II decision makers, the DMO, the CVB, and tourism authorities, to maximize attendance and ensure success. To this extent, DCCs are one degree removed from their final consumer market, so marketing staff must work in collaboration to promote the convention to a third level of decision makers–potential delegates, employers, and, increasingly, their families.

Singapore has provided the model for marketing conventions and events collaboratively. The Singapore Tourism Board (STB) is a tourism marketing entity that is both a National Tourism Organisation (NTO) and a Convention and Visitors Bureau (CVB). Singapore convention marketing is primarily conducted by the STB through its Singapore Exhibition and Convention Bureau (SECB) division. The Trade Development Board (TDB) is also a significant global marketer of trade shows and exhibitions for Singapore. These organizations work collectively on various initiatives to further Singapore's reputation as a leading MICE (Meetings, Incentives, Conventions, and Exhibitions) destination that attracts over 400,000 international visitors to about 4,000 events and conventions annually. MacLaurin and Leong (2000) provide the example of the "Globalmeet" campaign, a combined effort by the STB and convention industry to market Singaporean convention services internationally. This trade show combined the efforts of hotels, attractions, freight forwarders, decorator contractors, and food and beverage providers to promote Singapore as a value-driven convention destination following the Asian economic downturn of 1997/1998.

Efforts to promote the Globalmeet campaign began in 1997 when the TDB created a blueprint for Singapore to become an International Exhibition City (IEC). In conjunction with the newly formed private sector Exhibition Management Services, a task force with 40 major players developed and promoted both the hardware and the software components concurrently to improve services and conveniences to exhibitors and visitors of trade shows held in Singapore. Promotional strategies included sales missions to overseas markets, an incentive program to bring in international convention service buyers, as well as familiarization trips to convince professional conference organizers to choose Singapore. This promotion capitalized on Singapore's three major competitive advantages, namely hotel services, air access, and hotel rooms. These competitive advantages are also cited by Oppermann (1996) as being important factors in the convention site selection process. These features were influential in the Singapore International Convention and Exhibition Centre (SICEC) hosting 20,000 delegates at the Rotary International convention in 1999 (Yap, 1999), the largest meeting ever to be hosted in Southeast Asia.

It is evident from this literature review that there are a number of issues in the global conventions and exhibitions sector that provide the context for a case study of the development of a DCC in Perth, WA. These issues are outlined below under the headings of feasibility and funding; design, location, and construction; and operations, management, and marketing.

FUNDING, FINANCE, AND FEASIBILITY

A dedicated convention center for Western Australia was first mooted in the mid-1980s. But it wasn't until July 1991 that the Perth Convention Bureau (PCB), a WA government division of the Western Australian Tourism Commission (WATC), produced a pre-feasibility study to determine whether a full feasibility study should be undertaken. The study found that conventions are an important and growing area of tourism in WA and the economic benefits in the form of delegate expenditure are more than double other visitor types. It was also claimed that conventions inject AU$34 million annually into the WA economy and international conventions have a substantial effect on balance of payments. Conventions were found to be effective in generating additional visitors to Australia who would not otherwise have visited.

Perth in the early 1990s was suited to conferences up to 500 delegates but had logistical problems with larger conventions. There was a limited number of venues for large conventions, with the Burswood Resort and the Perth Concert Hall as the only large capacity venues. However, neither of these had all of the facilities required in a DCC. The study also described the need for Perth to "have an alignment of total room capacity, transport systems, and other infrastructure to support a DCC" (Perth Convention Bureau, 1991, p. 3). The recommendations of the pre-feasibility study proposed that two options were available to the government: either negotiate with Burswood Resort to include additional conventions capacity as part of its future expansion plans or complete a full feasibility study of a new DCC or extension of an existing public building. Therein a tension between public and private interests was created that was to contribute to a prolonged DCC development process that lasted for over a decade. These public-private partnership (PPP) arrangements, where the provision of public infrastructure is contracted to the private sector, are extremely complex and highly politicized. Yet there is some evidence that in some circumstances they deliver benefits in terms of efficiency, service provision, monitoring, and accountability as well as instilling higher levels of investor confidence (Hodge, 2002).

Debate over this public-private partnership arrangement led to the commissioning of an independent feasibility study in 1994 (Pannell Kerr Forster Consulting, 1994). The study found that the main factors in the selection of a convention destination were choice, availability, and suitability of venues, including hotels. Perth was limited to the smaller-scale end of the meetings market, with infrastructure, including airline services, being the main obstacle to the larger scale convention. The report recognized the need to develop proposals for new hotels and to expand airline capacity in response to growth in tourism in Western Australia. With regards to the capacity of the proposed DCC, the study recommended a plenary hall of 2,500 seats, with equivalent breakout rooms and banquet capacity, an exhibition hall of 10,000 square meters, and car parking for 600 cars.

Most importantly, the study found that Burswood was the most economical investment approach when compared with three other CBD development options. These were the Busport site, Northbridge, and the Perth Concert Hall. The costs for developing a DCC on each of these sites was estimated at AU$146 million for the Busport, AU$157 million for Northbridge, AU$110 million for Perth Concert Hall, and AU$36 million for Burswood.

The economic impact for a DCC was estimated to be AU$9.8 million in the first year, increasing to AU$20.5 million in year five. The DCC was expected to turn a profit for the state by year four of operation with a fifth year profit of almost AU$1 million on turnover of AU$1.2 billion (Table 1). However, a warning was given that management and marketing arrangements must commence immediately in order to achieve the best possible result on opening.

Again, there was considerable delay in deciding between a public-owned and funded DCC development and the privately funded development at Burswood. The delay was only exacerbated by the realization that the public cost of a DCC would be in the order of AU$150 million and that Burswood was planning to expand its convention facilities to capitalize on the growth Perth had experienced in the smaller convention market in the 1990s. After a further three-year delay in reaching a development decision, an updated feasibility study was undertaken (Tourism Co-ordinates, nd). A general economic overview described the health of the West Australian economy and how economic growth continued to out-pace that of other states, influenced by strong economic activity in the Asian region. The state of the tourism industry was

TABLE 1. Estimated Five-Year Returns to a DCC Development in AUD

	Revenues AU$	Profit (Loss) AU$	Cash Flow AU$
Year 1	9,781,000	(1,688,000)	(927,000)
Year 2	12,608,000	(937,000)	(317,000)
Year 3	15,558,000	(153,000)	319,000
Year 4	18,385,000	520,000	851,000
Year 5	20,546,000	996,000	1,219,000

Source: Pannell Kerr Forster Consulting, 1994.

also described as being very positive, with a new destination branding strategy, impending international exposure of Australia during the Sydney 2000 Olympics, privatization of Perth Airport, continued economic growth in Asia, improved air services, and planned capital investment in tourism for Western Australia auguring well for WA tourism in the mid-1990s.

The updated feasibility study described how the competition between states for convention business had grown since the 1994 study was completed, with extensions to facilities in Melbourne and Sydney having implications for the proposed Perth DCC. Perth was described as being in a position where it could not compete for conventions with Sydney, Melbourne, and Brisbane and was not even able to match Cairns, Adelaide, or Canberra. Despite these constraints, Perth had increased its share of national meetings from 10.61% in 1994 to 18.09% in 1996, and demand for national meetings was forecast to grow. However, a major inhibiting factor for Perth was that 70% of corporate head offices were located in the eastern states' cities of Sydney and Melbourne, which offered a wider range of convention facilities, air services, and hotel accommodation.

The 1997 study posed two options for a DCC, one public and one private: Northbridge and Burswood. Northbridge was recommended due to its proximity to the Perth CBD, and Burswood was recommended because of the advantages of lower investment costs to develop the required level of facilities. Burswood recognized that the government was under considerable pressure from the tourism industry to develop a DCC and that it could attempt to leverage considerable government support for a public-private funded facility at Burswood.

The update study also reviewed the management structure and agreed with the 1994 report (Pannell Kerr Forster Consulting, 1994) that a "management structure based on an executive team operating under the control of a commercially adept government-appointed board" (p. 14) be put in place if Northbridge is the chosen option. If Burswood is selected, the management issues are described as being more complex due to it being a combined public-private investment. It was suggested that if Burswood was selected, an industry consultative committee structure might be put into place to manage the public-private partnership in the DCC.

By the late 1990s, it had become apparent that no facility, public or private, would be developed without a substantial public investment. This was not forthcoming until the 1998/1999 WA government budget was set in place. Additional government revenues of AU$2.4 billion had become available after the government sold a gas pipeline to private sector interests. Subsequent to this sale, a budget allocation of AU$100 million was announced for construction of a new dedicated convention center for Perth. While this allocation of public funds was criticized in government and commercial circles, claiming that the funds would be better spent on a new public transport system, the then WA premier (The Honourable Richard Court) argued that the new center would generate a return of AU$2.2 billion over 10 years and create 140 permanent jobs and 450 casual jobs (Thomas, 2002).

To this end, the government announced an incentive package of up to AU$100 million and the provision of Crown Land (land vested in the government) for the development of the Perth Convention and Exhibition Center (PCEC). After a call for expressions of interest from three consortia, a full proposal was requested from the preferred provider, Multiplex Constructions Pty Ltd. A special purpose development vehicle (Perth CEC Pty Ltd.) was established, and a project agreement was struck whereby the government loaned the development vehicle AU$100 million (Net Present Value at July 2000) toward the construction cost of the center. Under the complex loan agreement, in effect, the 35-year loan can be repaid by transfer of ownership of the PCEC to the state government. Also under the loan agreement, the developer is required to build a hotel on the Busport site and comply with construction milestones during the 30-month construction phase of the project. Total investment in the PCEC project, including both the private and public investments, amounts to more than AU$220 million. Interestingly, the major shareholder in the Burswood Convention Center (the Wyllie Group of Companies) has invested AU$60 million in the PCEC, replacing Multiplex as the major private sector partner and facilitating a good working relationship between the PCEC and the existing casino, convention, and resort facility in Perth. The main components of the PCEC which are expected to be completed by mid-2004 were:

- a 17,000 square meter exhibition center, including a flexible space for performing arts.
- a convention center accommodating up to 2,500 people, with a banquet facility to be built above the convention center to seat up to 2,500 people.

One final delay in the approval process occurred in 2001, following a change of government in Western Australia. A brief period of contract re-negotiation was entered into to create more certainty about construction milestones for the center, the hotel, the car park, and the office space components of the project. Construction of a sports stadium that was also included in the previous contract arrangement was abandoned. By May 2001, the Cabinet decided to "advise Multiplex Constructions Pty Ltd. of the government's intention to be bound by the conditions of the Project Agreement(s) entered into by the previous government and that it expects Multiplex Constructions Pty Ltd. to be equally bound" (Boelen, personal communication, November 8, 2002), and construction commenced immediately. Ironically, exactly a decade had passed between the first pre-feasibility and the commencement of construction.

DESIGN, LOCATION, AND CONSTRUCTION

In 2000, an extensive industry consultation process was established within the government to identify preferred location, design, and construction specifications. To facilitate public input into the design process, a website was established where preferred sites could be nominated. A government working group comprised of representatives from the public service and the conventions and events industry in WA set about developing a Project Agreement Document for the PCEC. This agreement set the design, location, and physical parameters of the PCEC and detailed the preferred management structure.

The preferred location was the Busport site, located at the northern end of the city and adjacent to the Swan River, parklands, and the freeway interchange. There are also a number of hotels within walking distance of the site, as well as plans for additional hotel accommodation on site. A major new hotel development adjacent to the site has been postponed, repeating the U.S. experience that hotel development tends to lag behind DCC development (Casey, 1998). While these lag periods limit the ability of the destination to attract conventions, they are also understandable given that large projects have a distorting effect on the labor market for all forms of construction trades, forcing up the cost of projects. For example, the PCEC engaged every ground plumber in Perth during the early stages of construction. It makes commercial sense to avoid competing for limited construction services when large projects are underway.

Design of the PCEC involved the use of the latest technology and engineering available in Australia to ensure that access, capacity, and internal and external appearance were optimized. According to the PCEC website on October 31, 2002, the Perth Convention and Exhibition Center is being constructed by Multiplex Constructions Pty Ltd., one of Australia's largest development and construction companies. Multiplex built Stadium Australia, the Sydney 2000 Olympic Games venue, as well as many major facilities in WA. Multiplex has taken considerable equity in the PCEC and will also construct an office and hotel building on the site, taking their total private investment to AU$250 million. Under the terms of the contract, ownership of the PCEC will revert to the government after 35 years (Thomas, 2002).

OPERATIONS, MANAGEMENT, AND MARKETING

In 2001, PCEC operating rights were sold by Multiplex to a private company, Spotless Facilities (hereafter "the operators"), for a 10-year period. The operators will run the facility as a commercial concern, in a management fee plus profit-share relationship, reviewed after 5 years. As the operator, it will also be subject to performance assessment against a set of key performance indicators (KPIs) based on additional economic impact, bed nights, and tourism activity. To this end, the operators have put in place a hotel relationship charter with some 26 accommodation establishments in Perth to make certain that attractive and price competitive convention accommodation packages are available to PCOs, decision makers, and delegates. This will ensure that Perth remains competitive with convention centers on the east coast of Australia and that it will continue to attract national and international conventions and trade shows. During operation, the operators will outsource the functional areas of catering, cleaning, sales and marketing, security, and car parking to local companies and employ about 20 core staff and a part-time staff of approximately 400 persons.

The important task of national and international sales and marketing of the PCEC was subcontracted to a private company, V3. This company works closely with the operators and the Perth Convention Bureau to identify, bid for, and attract national and international convention business for Perth. Under this arrangement, the PCEC has secured 95 bookings–2 years before the center is even due to open. These bookings, out to 2009, are forecast to generate 70,000 visitor nights in Perth and an additional AU$87 million in economic impact. This will, of course, go some way to recovering the cost of public investment in the project. By way of comparison, the Brisbane Convention and Exhibition Center (BCEC) had secured some 200 bookings, including 37 national and international conventions, two years before opening in 1995 (Anonymous, 1993). These bookings were forecast to generate AU$72 million for the Queensland economy, and the BCEC expected to generate more than AU$1 billion over a decade for Queensland. In both of these forecasts, there is no mention of the extent of the substitution effect within state economic activity, nor is there an estimate of the opportunity cost of the AU$170 million of public funds invested in 1993 by the Queensland government.

CONCLUSION

From the preceding review of issues and case study of the PCEC, it is apparent that construction of dedicated convention facilities is an extremely complex process involving public and private agencies in detailed arrangements for funding, design, construction, operation, and marketing. In this regard, DCCs present a unique opportunity to investigate this type of public-private sector partnerships (PPP) at all stages of development and across all levels of government. Many convention centers around the world have some level of public and private sector involvement. Furthermore, unlike other development projects in construction, mining, or public infrastructure, public involvement continues after the construction phase is complete, and DCCs rarely revert to private sector ownership and control. The reasons for this are evident and are based on the following general points:

1. DCCs rarely turn a profit as a stand-alone facility due to the high capital cost of construction and operation.
2. Competition between DCCs is increasing around the world as new and established convention destinations construct new facilities.
3. Additional investment is required for extensions, additions, and refurbishments as the size of conventions and exhibitions increases over time.
4. The conventions business is global in nature, exposing it to impacts of economic recession in major markets, terrorism, and uncertainty over security of travel.

For these reasons, governments must always consider DCCs as public goods–in that they generate returns to the wider community as a result of public investment in the same way that public schools and hospitals do. The difference being that whereas schools and hospitals provide essential services, conventions business and tourism are considered non-essential activities in the public sector. However, it should be recognized that conventions and business tourism are vital tools for education, marketing, networking, and corporate communications and, therefore, play an important role in the economy. In competing for public funds they are subject to intense scrutiny during the feasibility and design stage, as was the case in Western Australia where three studies over 5 years were undertaken to investigate the financial, locational, design, and operational aspects of the PCEC.

Financing of DCCs will always involve public funds that can be structured in a number of ways, including loans, bonds, or grants. In addition, public lands are often made available for DCCs, given the prime need to be located in a prominent or landmark site which links with the city's major natural and cultural features. These funding arrangements give rise to unique and complex public-private partnership arrangements that are subject to public probity processes and private sector profit imperatives.

The design and construction of DCCs become critical elements in the development process due to the prominence of the site and the internal design requirements of major conventions and exhibitions (such as access and column-free exhibition space). This leads to innovative roof engineering, which often becomes an iconic external feature of the DCC; for example, the roof of the PCEC is designed to resemble an Australian native gum-tree leaf in shape and contour. Internally, meeting room requirements have been specified to accommodate several thousand delegates in plenary and breakout format, and the associated banqueting facilities must match the capacity of the meeting rooms, as must the adjacent accommodation, parking, and transport capacity.

It is critical in marketing DCCs that cooperative arrangements are put in place between the center and private marketing agencies, public destination management organizations, city convention bureaux, and federal tourism marketing agencies. In some cases, including the PCEC, management and marketing of DCCs have been contracted out to private agencies, extending the network of public and private partnership to the operational stage. It is imperative that pre-marketing activities lock in bookings well in advance of opening, to minimize "down" or "black" time in the first few years after opening. Incidentally, this pre-booking of conventions and meetings places additional pressure on construction milestones and the need to avoid delays in opening. After several years of operation, it has been the experience of convention centers that addition, renovation, or refurbishment is necessary, again raising the requirement to source public and private funds. In many ways, then, development of dedicated convention facilities is a cyclical rather than an iterative process that presents a range of issues for ongoing investigation by researchers and practitioners alike.

REFERENCES

Anonymous. (1993, October/November). Convention centre gives Brisbane international focus. *Kurilpa. Newsletter of the Brisbane Convention and Exhibition Centre, 1*(1), 1.

Carlsen, J. (1999). A review of MICE industry evaluation and research in Asia and Australia 1988-1998. *Journal of Convention and Exhibition Management, 1*(4), 51-66.

Carlsen, J. (2002, March 28-April 3). Tourism spin-off an appealing outcome. *Business News*, 17.

Casey, R. (1998). Hopes and Dreams. *Successful Meetings, 47*(10), 50.

Harris, E. E. (1999). Convention centers lure investors along with city planners. *Bond Buyer, 327*, 8.

Hiller, H. (1995). Conventions as mega-events. A new model for host-host city relationships. *Tourism Management, 16*(5), 375-379.

Hodge, G. (2002). Who steers the state when governments sign public-private partnerships? *Journal of Contemporary Issues in Business and Government, 8*(1), 5-18.

Johnson, L., Foo, L. M., & O'Halloran, M. (1999). *Meetings make their mark. Characteristics and economic contribution of Australia's meetings and exhibitions sector* (Occasional Paper Number 26). Canberra, Australia: Bureau of Tourism Research.

Law, C. M. (1996). *Tourism in major cities*. London: International Thomson Business Press.

MacLaurin, D., & Leong, K. (2000). Strategies for success: How Singapore attracts and retains the convention and trade show industry. *Event Management, 6*(3), 93-103.

McCabe, V., Poole, B., Weeks, P., & Leiper, N. (2000). *The business and management of conventions*. Queensland, Australia: Wiley.

Meany, R. (2002). Size matters. *Successful Meetings, 51*(10), 125.

Oppermann, M. (1996). Convention destination images: Analysis of association meeting planner's perceptions. *Tourism Management, 17*(3), 175-182.

Pannell Kerr Forster Consulting. (1994). *A feasibility study to determine the viability of a dedicated convention and exhibition centre for Perth, Western Australia*. Unpublished report.

Perth Convention and Exhibition Centre. Retrieved October 31, 2002, from http://www.pcecwa.com.au/

Perth Convention Bureau. (1991). *Pre-feasibility study to determine whether a feasibility study should be undertaken for a dedicated convention centre in Perth*. Unpublished report.

Perth Convention Bureau. (2000). Western Australia MICE report. Perth, Australia: Perth Convention Bureau.

Reisman, M. (1999). Florida high court clears path for Osceoila convention center. *Bond Buyer, 328*, 1-4.

Rutherford, D. G. (1990). Introduction to the conventions, expositions and meetings industry. New York: Van Nostrand Reinhold.

Sandilands, B. (1993, April 20). Conventions special report. *The Bulletin*, 23.

Thomas, G. (2002, September 16). Conventions bookings flow. *The West Australian*, 4.

Tourism Co-ordinates. (nd). Dedicated convention exhibition centre Perth feasibility update. Unpublished report.

Turkel, S. (2002). Convention-center growth requires better feasibility studies. *Hotel and Motel Management, 217*(11), 61.

Wirtz, R. A. (2001). Stadiums and convention centers as community loss leaders. *Fedgazette, 13*(2), 5-7.

Yap, E. (1999, June 14). S'pore's biggest meet gets off to a good start. *The Straits Times*, p. 3.

Casinos and Conventions: Strange Bedfellows

George G. Fenich, PhD
Kathryn Hashimoto, PhD

SUMMARY. The casino industry has always relied on the leisure traveler whose primary motivation is to gamble. Thus, one would expect the casino and convention industries to operate in totally different arenas. This was the case until the mid-1990s. Today, the casino industry is embracing the convention industry and constructing facilities to meet the needs of the convention and meeting attendee. This article starts by setting up the framework for this dichotomy between the two industries by tracing the history of casino gaming in the U.S. Discussion leads to a review of how and why there was a lack of conventions/meetings business in both Las Vegas and Atlantic City. The article then goes on to review specific development of the conventions/meetings business in Las Vegas, Atlantic City, and other jurisdictions. It concludes with a prognosis about the future along with opportunities for future research. *[Article copies available for a fee from The Haworth Document Delivery Service: 1-800-HAWORTH. E-mail ad-*

George G. Fenich is Professor, Lester E. Kabacoff School of Hotel, Restaurant, and Tourism Administration, University of New Orleans.

Kathryn Hashimoto is Assistant Professor, Lester E. Kabacoff School of Hotel, Restaurant, and Tourism Administration, University of New Orleans.

Address correspondence to either author at: The Lester E. Kabacoff School of Hotel, Restaurant, and Tourism Administration, University of New Orleans, Lakefront Campus, New Orleans, LA 70148.

[Haworth co-indexing entry note]: "Casinos and Conventions: Strange Bedfellows." Fenich, George G., and Kathryn Hashimoto. Co-published simultaneously in *Journal of Convention & Event Tourism* (The Haworth Hospitality Press, an imprint of The Haworth Press, Inc.) Vol. 6, No. 1/2, 2004, pp. 63-79; and: *Current Issues in Convention and Exhibition Facility Development* (ed: Robert R. Nelson) The Haworth Hospitality Press, an imprint of The Haworth Press, Inc., 2004, pp. 63-79. Single or multiple copies of this article are available for a fee from The Haworth Document Delivery Service [1-800-HAWORTH, 9:00 a.m. - 5:00 p.m. (EST). E-mail address: docdelivery@haworthpress.com].

http://www.haworthpress.com/web/JCET
Digital Object Identifier: 10.1300/J452v06n01_05

dress: <docdelivery@haworthpress.com> Website: <http://www.HaworthPress.com> © 2004 by The Haworth Press, Inc. All rights reserved.]

KEYWORDS. Conventions, casinos, physical development, Las Vegas, Atlantic City, Native American

INTRODUCTION

The casino industry has always relied on the leisure traveler whose primary motivation is to gamble for most of its business. In the past, the industry elicited images of mega-resorts, top notch entertainment, inexpensive buffet meals, comp rooms, and people who gamble all night while sleeping all day. None of the foregoing dovetails with the psychographics and demographics of convention/meeting attendees. The latter are in meetings all day, want a nice dinner, are not particularly price conscious about rooms, and tend to be conservative with their money. Thus, one would expect the casino and convention industries to operate in totally different arenas. This was the case until the mid-1990s.

In spite of their large number of rooms, name entertainers, casino operations, and things to do while meetings were not in session, casinos did not capitalize on their attractiveness for meetings and conventions. The casino and convention industries did not connect. "Keep in mind that Las Vegas has changed so dramatically in such a short period of time. Its perception is beyond the Las Vegas of 10 or even 5 years ago. The consumer, as we see him or her, is not the stereotype that many still believe come here" (Bulavsky, 1999, p. 57). Today the casino industry is embracing the convention industry and constructing facilities to meet the needs of the convention and meeting attendee. "From the glitzy boulevards of Las Vegas to the lower reaches of the Mississippi Delta, properties that woo groups on the twin strengths of convention facilities and casinos are multiplying and expanding at a rapid rate" (Cooke, 2000, p. 52).

This article starts by setting up the framework for this dichotomy between the two industries by tracing the history of casino gaming in the United States. Discussion leads to a review of how and why there was a lack of conventions/meetings business in both Las Vegas and Atlantic City. This began to change as gambling expanded into new jurisdictions and casino operators explored other sources of business. These operators realized that conventions/meetings were an ideal source of new business and began to embrace this market. The article then goes on to review specific development of the conventions/meetings business in Las Vegas, Atlantic City, and other jurisdictions. It concludes with a prognosis about the future.

HISTORY OF THE CASINO INDUSTRY

Las Vegas

The epicenter for casino gaming is in Las Vegas, Nevada, where legal casino gambling has existed since the 1920s. However, nationwide awareness of Las Vegas as a gaming mecca did not occur until the 1940s, when a gangster, Bugsy Siegel, opened a full-scale resort, the Flamingo. Much of this notoriety was based on Siegel's success in attracting actors, actresses, and movie stars to the resort. These were the type of people Las Vegas wanted to attract: leisure travelers with high discretionary incomes (whales) whose primary interest was gambling. This, in turn, motivated other leisure tourists, who wanted the same excitement and to be seen with famous people, to flock to Las Vegas.

The people operating casinos had ties to organized crime. Thus, their reputations precluded them from being involved with traditional business people. Legislation of the era required that an individual, not a corporation, own the casino. As a result, traditional American business, and business travelers, shunned casinos along with Las Vegas itself. Conventions and meetings did not go to Las Vegas. In part, this was due to the conservative nature of the convention/meeting traveler along with the distain mainstream America had for gambling, and thus Las Vegas. Church-going Americans did not gamble!

Additionally, the Las Vegas casino operator did not want the meeting or convention traveler. And over the years, meeting planners have felt that the casino hotels would rather keep their rooms available for any high rollers who might come into town. Everything the casino did was based on the viewpoint that visitors must be involved in gambling for most of their visit. This was due to the widely held belief of the time that a casino could only be successful if it derived virtually all its revenue from the casino floor. The operators wanted to attract gamblers by offering complimentary rooms, food, shows, transportation, and so forth. They made their money through the long hours these people spent at the gaming tables and the large bets they made. Given the tradition of giving "comps" to patrons, the operators rationalized that they did not want patrons who gambled little and spent their days in meetings rather than on the casino floor. "There was a long period when the leadership of the casino industry did not subscribe to the importance of the convention trade" (Ghitelman, 1997, p. 79).

As Las Vegas casinos grew in size and number, the operators realized they had a problem attracting capital and they needed Wall Street stockbrokers to help fund their endeavors. However, the history of casinos looking to organized crime as their largest source of funds was a detriment. This changed in 1969 when the Corporate Gaming Act in Nevada allowed corporations to own and operate casinos. One of the first and best known "legitimate business people" to develop a presence in Las Vegas casinos was Howard Hughes, through his aircraft company. As more legitimate corporations, under scrutiny of the S.E.C., bought casinos, the American public became more accepting of gambling–as long as it remained in "someone else's back yard." Las Vegas was the only place in the United States where one could legally gamble. Thus, Las Vegas could rely on attracting the very narrow market of serious gamblers. The meetings and conventions segment was largely shunned by the casino operators. There are many stories about conventioneers arriving in Las Vegas only to find that the casino had arbitrarily canceled their room reservations because regular gamblers had shown up at the last minute.

The casinos in Nevada, largely Las Vegas, operated without any competition until 1978. That is the year that legalized casinos began in Atlantic City and removed Las Vegas' monopoly power. While it was only the second jurisdiction in the United States to allow casino gaming, the operators in Las Vegas were concerned about loss of business through cannibalization. This set the stage for consideration of sources of business other than the traditional leisure traveler who was a serious gambler.

Atlantic City

Atlantic City is located on an island off the coast of New Jersey in the eastern United States. During its long history, it has served as a recreational seashore attraction, even for American Indians in pre-colonial times. However, since it is located in the northeast United States, its seashore tourism season only lasted a few months, from Memorial Day to Labor Day. Interestingly enough, Atlantic City was one of the first locales to use a special event to lengthen its "season." That event is the Miss America Contest, which takes place in mid-September every year. Even though the event hall (convention hall) was built to house the contest, the hotel and resort operators in Atlantic City made little use of it for events other than the contest. After all, as early as the 1920s, Atlantic City was a very successful tourist destination and one of the few linked by rail to the large population centers of the northeastern United States.

However, with advances in automobile and air transportation after the Second World War, Atlantic City saw a decline in its core "seashore" business and did try to attract meetings and conventions during the shoulder seasons (most hotels still closed from late fall through spring, in part, due to lack of heat). This business segment grew, but the community and its infrastructure did not–in fact, it went into decline. According to Marshall Murdaugh, the executive director of the Atlantic City CVB, "We were a major meeting site 50 years ago. The market has changed since then, and our place in it slowly and consistently diminished" (as cited in Ghitelman, 1997, p. 81). The authors of this article recollect attending the statewide teachers' convention in Atlantic City in 1976. The city was dirty, grungy, and attendees felt unsafe walking between the event hall and hotels at night. Further, there was nothing to do in the off-season, when it was too cold for the beach. The city fathers tried to rejuvenate their tourism business by hosting a national political convention in the mid-1970s, but it backfired. The convention was boring, so reporters searched the city for news stories. Consequently, reporters began to refer to Atlantic City as "the slum by the sea." It was after that convention that the famous phrase "Would the last person to leave Atlantic City please shut off the lights" was coined. Even a convention could not save the troubled city. The city needed a catalyst for redevelopment.

The Advent of Casino Gaming

That catalyst came with the legalization of casino gaming in Atlantic City in 1976 and the opening of Resorts Casino Hotel in 1978. The legislation mandated that all casinos be integral parts of full-service hotels. However, the pattern of physical development and business followed that of Las Vegas. This is not surprising since virtually all of the casino operators came from Las Vegas and, thus, had the Las Vegas mindset: attract high rollers who will spend money on the casino floor. They believed that the only path to success and profits lay in generating revenue on the casino floor. Even with increasing competition as more casinos opened in Atlantic City, the operators still looked to the casino floor for revenues. Given that the location was within driving distance of one-third of the population of the United States, this led to development of the low-roller, high-volume bus business. Many players also drove to Atlantic City, spent hundreds of dollars, and were weekly visitors. These new target markets had one thing in common: they all came to gamble as their primary recreation. Like in Las Vegas, the convention/meeting attendee was not even on the radar screen of the operators since the attendee did not fit the demographic and psychographic profile of the casino patron.

The Lack of Convention Business in Pre-1990 Gaming Destinations

Nevada, and especially Las Vegas, had never tried to attract the convention/meeting business. They were always too focused on satisfying their gaming players to worry about customers who were considered "fringe" players. At one point, Atlantic City planners started to develop a reasonably strong–albeit short–convention/meeting season, but they let it slip through their hands due to infrastructure deterioration. As was discussed earlier, casino operators never really bought into the concept. However, gamblers in Atlantic City usually come on the weekends. Therefore, casinos considered filling some rooms with conventioneers, but only in mid-week. "Traditionally, the big hotels are forced to offer mid-week bargain packages to fill rooms Monday through Thursday. This of course affects bottom line" (Shemeligian, 1999, p. 57). But 100% occupancy of the hotel was never the main objective. Hotel rooms were not considered a profit center but rather as free gifts to good gamblers. For example, none of the suites at Harrah's Las Vegas, with a stated value of $5,000 per night or more, are ever rented to cash-paying customers. They are always kept in reserve to be given, free of charge, to gamblers with a credit line rating in excess of $1 million. This is obviously based on the belief that revenues and profits come solely off the casino floor.

Casino managers who considered hosting a convention/meeting would only do so during their slowest periods, when they felt it was impossible to attract the core gambler. Thus, at best, some might consider a mid-week meeting, so long as it did not take place during peak or shoulder gaming seasons. In Atlantic City, this meant conventions/meetings were relegated to the winter months when chilling temperatures and howling winds made it very unpleasant to even be in Atlantic City. The authors recollect scheduling a national conference in Atlantic City during early January. A major snowstorm blew in that paralyzed the city for 3 days and wreaked havoc with the meeting. In Las Vegas, meetings were only scheduled in the few weeks before Christmas or in June, before the summer travelers hit.

Atlantic City developed the day-trip bus business to the point where there were more busses running in Atlantic City than any other city except New York. Both Las Vegas and Atlantic City also focused on "comps," which is short for "complimentary." They gave free or discounted meals, along with hotel rooms, transportation, and so forth, to patrons who were "rated gamblers." And these comps were given in direct relation to the rating: the higher the rating, the greater the comps. This approach supported the business practice of trying to increase market share solely through additional gamblers and not other market segments. Further, casino operators believed that convention/meeting attendees were not good for business. "I have actually been told in so many words, 'We don't need your business' says Debbie Hubler . . . of the National Cattlemen's Beef Association in Englewood, Colorado" (Finney, 1997, p. 65).

Casino managers could not even envision offsetting lower gaming revenues from convention/meeting attendees with higher room rates or food and beverage business. They did not have to worry about such "out of the box thinking" until the early 1990s. That is because, until that time, there were only two places with legal casino gaming and, therefore, they had an oligopoly situation. That changed in the early 1990s with the legalization of casino gaming in many additional jurisdictions along with growth in Native American gaming. "We have had all these rooms, and we haven't been able to migrate to the high price midweek segment. The convention business has been starkly missing from our customer profile" (Palermo, 2002, p. 34).

Gambling Expands

By the 1990s, the two meccas of casino gaming had competition that caused concern for existing operators. There was concern about the increase in competition from new gaming jurisdictions across the country and a concern among casino operators that in the near future, the vast majority of states would have legalized casino gaming. There was also a fear of the potential market saturation for gaming. Adding to this problem was the fact that both Atlantic City and especially Las Vegas were increasing the number of casinos and hotel rooms, thus creating internal competition. This forced operators to become competitive and look for other sources of business. For example, Las Vegas tried to reinvent itself as a family destination, constructing such facilities as Circus Circus, the MGM Grand with its theme park and *Wizard of Oz* theme, and Treasure Island with its pirates. But it did not work, and this strategy has now been abandoned. Atlantic City tried, early on, to build its base through bus trippers, but these patrons did not patronize the restaurants let alone fill the hotel rooms. None of the strategies they tried were particularly successful.

LAS VEGAS AND ATLANTIC CITY LOOK TO CONVENTIONS

Gaming destinations have only recently begun to look to the convention and meeting segment as a significant source of business and revenue.

> And within a chips' throw of every gaming mecca lies a convention center–the distant cousin to the nuclear family of gambling tourism. Everybody knows they are related, but they just cannot quite agree as to how. It's an uneasy relationship, at best. Gambling destinations are pouring millions into new or expanded convention centers. But across the years, meeting planners have felt as if they have been tossed the table scraps by the surrounding hotels that would really rather keep their rooms available just in case a high roller should stumble in. (Finney, 1997, p. 64)

Additionally, as casino operations became more corporate in their workings, they "crunched the numbers" to ascertain opportunities. They found that conventions and meetings could be a good source of business. It was realized that these attendees had larger pocketbooks and were not as sensitive to rate as leisure travelers. Thus, casino hotels could charge attendees a higher room rate than leisure based gamblers and counteract the lower gaming activity of those attendees. Further supporting the value of the convention/meeting business were revenues channeled through the food and beverage department. Unlike the leisure gambler, conventions/meetings would spend money on full priced food and beverage and the convention/meeting sponsor would pay for banquets, receptions, coffee breaks, and more. The companies that exhibit at trade shows spend huge amounts entertaining attendees/clients at hospitality suites, elaborate dinners, and receptions. After all, the average convention delegate spends $968 in the community during the convention, while convention sponsors spend an additional $73 per delegate for a total of $1,041 (Hanson, 2002). The "number crunchers" of casino corporations determined that conventions/meetings could generate more, in the aggregate, than the average gambler. Corporate headquarters convinced the property manager of the importance of the convention/meeting segment. Further supporting the embracing of conventions by the casino industry is the fact that Nevada generated exhibit spending of almost one billion dollars in 2001 and ranks fourth of all states in the United States in terms of total exhibit space (Center for Exhibition Industry Research, 2002).

Conventions/meetings are a good source of business for casinos because they complement, not compete with, the leisure gambler. Gamblers prefer to frequent casinos on weekends, holidays, and summer periods, just like most leisure travelers. By contrast, conventions/meetings rarely start their program prior to Monday and prefer to culminate activities by Thursday so their attendees can be at home with families on the weekends. The same holds true for holidays and summers: most groups do not meet then. As a result, conventions/meetings fit nicely with the ebb and flow of casino clientele.

THE CASE OF FACILITIES DEVELOPMENT IN LAS VEGAS

Even though Las Vegas has been a travel destination since, at least, the 1940s, the boom in convention/meeting business, with its commensurate construction, did not take off until the mid-1990s. Nothing would make casinos happier, says John Yaskin, vice president of sales and marketing for Caesars Palace hotel and casino, than if "executives could close every sales office and fill every room with gamblers, but that isn't reality. And so, in order to fill premium rooms and suites with high-end clientele, the casino markets to convention and business travelers" (as cited in Shemeligian, 1999, p. 58). "While casino operators have clearly not abandoned the high roller and individual tourist markets, many are making concerted efforts to cultivate the meeting business with incentives and other initiatives" (Ross, 2000, p. 74). This is a distinct change since, until recently, all but two Las Vegas "casino operators have considered meetings only as midweek filler when business is low. Now everyone is realizing there are dollars in the market" (Nigro, 1998, p. 60).

New or Expanded Facilities

Many existing casino hotels are adding, expanding, or renovating their convention/meeting space. Bally's began renovation by updating its 180,000 square feet of meeting space followed by their guest rooms. Caesars Palace, once the exclusive haunt of high rollers, added 110,000 square feet of function space in 1997, while the MGM Grand hotel/casino (originally a leisure oriented *Wizard of Oz* theme) built a 380,000 square foot conference center in 1998 and in 2002 closed their theme park to all but convention groups. The Mirage, with 3,028 guest rooms, added a 90,000 square foot events center that brings their total meeting space to 172,000 square feet. Treasure Island, with its pirate theme, has installed high-speed Internet access using T-3 lines and is targeting conventioneers. The Texas Station added 35,000 square feet of meeting space including the 15,000 square foot Dallas Events Center. The Stardust has a total of 65,000 square feet of meeting space including the newly opened 40,000 square foot Pavilion and Exhibition Center (Baker, 2002; Cooke, 2000).

Many of the older, more traditional, casino hotels have incorporated convention/meeting space over the years. For example, the old stalwart in downtown, Binions, has 10,000 square feet of meeting space, the Golden Nugget has 35,000 and even the downscale El Cortez has 2,500. On the Strip, the family oriented Circus Circus has over 21,000 square feet of meeting space, Bugsy Siegel's Flamingo has 55,000, the Hard Rock Café and Hotel has 60,000, while the Riviera has 150,000 (Baker, 2002; Cooke, 2000).

Even some of the casino hotels built since the mid-1990s are adding convention/meeting space. Mandalay Bay Resort is adding a 1.8 million square foot convention center in an effort to level out the swings in their mid-week and weekend business (Berns, 2001). This is in addition to their existing 190,000 square foot conference center. Executives say "they would like to see 40% of their hotel business coming from conventioneers and trade show goers, rather than the current 21% that mix constitutes" (Berns, 2001, p. 1). The Aladdin, which was imploded to make way for the new facility, Desert Passage, opened in 1999 with 2,600 guest rooms and 75,000 square feet of meeting space. They also have a multi-purpose venue that seats 7,000 people. The 716-suite Tuscany hotel, which opened in 2001, is already adding 36,000 square feet of meeting space for a total of over 42,000. New York New York hotel and casino did renovations and expanded its meeting space from 12,000 to 15,000 square feet.

> The Venetian is the first hotel in the history of the world's entertainment capital to cater almost exclusively to the convention trade. All 3,000 rooms in the main tower are suites and all are linked to the 1.7 million square feet of space at the Sands Expo and Convention Center. (Shemeligian, 1999, p. 57)

The Sands Expo center is the largest privately owned convention facility in the country and one of the top five in total size. The Venetian itself was built with half a million square feet of meeting space and has almost completed an expansion adding 1,100 guest rooms and 75,000 square feet of meeting space (Cooke, 2000). "And I think the Venetian and Las Vegas are taking a share of the convention business from smaller cities like Nashville and Dallas" states Bank of America analyst Andrew Susser (Smith, 2003, p. 1).

The gaming impresario Steve Wynn is developing La Reve on the site of the former Desert Inn. It will have almost 2,500 guest rooms, a 132,000 square foot convention center (more floor space than their casino at 120,000) along with two entertainment venues with 1,500 and 2,000 seats, respectively.

Convention Center

The Las Vegas Convention Center sits blocks from the Strip and did not undergo any change since 1991, but saw a 300,000 square foot expansion in the late 1990s. Almost upon opening the expanded center, the Las Vegas Convention Authority announced still another expansion of 1.3 million square feet, which was completed in 2001. This was done to "further strengthen the city's reputation as the world's premier meeting and convention venue, according to Manny Cortez, president and CEO of the Authority" (Ross, 2000, p. 76).

Las Vegas Conventions and Attendance

Las Vegas has become the biggest convention city in the United States, surpassing Chicago and New York. Las Vegas has a total of about 4.5 million square feet of convention/meeting space and 125,000 hotel rooms. It also attracts six out of the ten largest trade shows based on net square feet utilized. It attracts the largest Trade Show, CONEXPO-CON/AGG, which uses 1.7 million square feet; the fourth largest, COMDEX, with 1.1 million; and the sixth largest, International CES, with 1.09 million. Las Vegas also captured four of the top ten Trade Shows ranked by the number of exhibitors including MAGIC/WWDMAGIC/MAGIC with 3,430 exhibiting companies. It also brought in three of the ten largest shows based on number of attendees, including the largest, COMDEX, with 200,000 (Shure, 2000).

By the year 2000, 3.85 million trade show and convention attendees visited Las Vegas, a 2.1% increase from the previous year. The economic impact of $4.3 billion showed a year to year increase of 4.2%. In that same year, it was found that conventioneers spent half a day longer than tourists at 4.1 nights compared to 3.7 nights. Further, trade show delegates spent an average of $1,273 on non-gaming items while conventioneers spent $961. This compares to only $630 for tourists (Berns, 2001). By 2001, Las Vegas attracted more than four million conventioneers with an economic impact of $4.8 billion. This increase was expected to continue with a projected 5.1% rise in 2002 (Baker, 2002).

In spite of these numbers and the appearance that the city is one of America's top convention and trade show destinations, Las Vegas could do much more. According to Sheldon Anderson, chairman of the Venetian Casino Hotel, Las Vegas has not yet tapped one-half of 1% of the convention business. "He said he battled with some Las Vegas officials about the importance of the convention business in past years and believes that business is now more important than ever as the city seeks to continually fill more hotel rooms" (Macy, 2000, p. 1).

THE CASE OF PHYSICAL DEVELOPMENT IN ATLANTIC CITY

As in Las Vegas, the casino/hotel operators in Atlantic City historically relied on the leisure gambler as the primary source of business. This occurred in spite of the fact that Atlantic City was one of the first municipalities to stage a national special event, the Miss America Pageant. The old mindset died hard, but it did change. In the late 1990s, Atlantic City operators, along with elected officials, decided to embrace the convention and meeting business. "Although casino development is the linchpin of Atlantic City's fortunes, the convention industry is critical to the city's growth, . . . according to Joe DiGirolamo, vice president of convention development for the Atlantic City Convention and Visitors Authority" (Grimaldi, 2000, p. 89). "There was a long period when the leadership of the casino industry did not subscribe to the importance of the convention trade" (Ghitelman, 1997, p. 79). Further, it was only in 1993 that the state-run Casino Reinvestment Authority began to offer financing for hotel construction, but only if operators would commit a percentage of those rooms for convention blocks (Nigro, 1998).

Probably the most significant physical development was the new convention center, meant to replace the aging event hall. The event hall was built in 1929 and was never designed as a convention or trade show venue. The new center opened in 1997 at a cost of $268 million with half a million square feet of space and 45 meeting rooms. It has more contiguous floor space than any competing convention center between Boston and Atlanta. Interestingly, it is not located on the boardwalk with the casinos, but is on the opposite side of the island at the foot of the Atlantic City Expressway and adjacent to the rail and bus terminal. A 500-room, non-casino hotel has been built next to the new center. It has 502 rooms, a 16,000 square foot ballroom, and 5,000 square feet of pre-function space. The Washington based association, NCEA, whose show attracts 14,000 attendees, exemplifies the previous lack or deterioration of the convention trade and the subsequent success of the center. They had not met in Atlantic City since 1975, but are moving their show back to the city because of its new center (Grimaldi, 2000).

Atlantic City has also seen a dearth of casino/hotel construction in the early 1990s. However, "the casino industry is now very aggressively developing Atlantic City's convention capacity" (Ghitelman, 1997 p. 80). The State of New Jersey decided to invest additional state resources in Atlantic City. They spent $265 million upgrading the convention center and $330 million in roadway improvements. However, the problem is room capacity. In 2003, Atlantic City had a 94.6% room occupancy rate with over 50% rooms comped. The high comping rate is due to the simple math: it is estimated that an overnight visitor will spend more than $400 per day on gambling whereas a day visitor spends only $100 (Klatzkin, 2003). Therefore, overnight tourists are in the best interests of the casino. However, originally, rooms were not part of the plans because casinos sought day trippers through bus programs. To address this issue in 1993, the legislators signed a law creating a $100 million pool of funds to add more hotel rooms, with an allowance of $150,000 per room so long as the casinos matched the funds. As a result, several casinos have expanded their hotel room inventory. In addition, the Borgata opened on July 3, 2003. It is a 1.1 billion dollar joint venture between Boyd Gaming and MGM Mirage and was the first new casino hotel to open in Atlantic City in 13 years. The property contains 2,002 hotel rooms, 11 restaurants, 11 retail shops, 2,400 seat event center, 1,000 seat performance theater, 125,000 square feet of gaming space, and 70,000 square feet of meeting space. Further, it will not be designed to accommodate trade shows; rather they will be directed to use the new convention center. However, even with the 4,100 new rooms, Atlantic City only has 15,276 rooms. The Atlantic City Convention Center has indicated the city needs 20,000 rooms to handle larger conventions. So while, the convention center is the largest single-level convention center on the East Coast, it lacks room availability to fully reach its potential.

Some of the existing properties are expanding with conventions/meetings in mind. Caesars underwent a $25 million expansion that added not only a guest room tower but 8,000 square feet of meeting space that can accommodate up to 2,000 delegates (Ross, 2000). Harrah's is also expanding with a new 450-room tower which will also have 30,500 square feet of meeting space, while the Tropicana is adding 502 rooms and 20,000 square feet of meeting space (Cooke, 2000). Bally's, in conjunction with Wild Wild West, is adding a boardwalk promenade that will include 8,000 square feet of meeting space.

Conventions and meetings had a significant impact on the economy of Atlantic City by the late 1990s. "In 1999, 300,000 convention and trade show attendees generated spending revenues of $214 million, a 73% increase over 1998" (Grimaldi, 2000, p. 88). In 2001, Atlantic City hosted 250 groups who occupied more than 50,000 room nights (Hardin, 2002). Thus, it is clear that after 20 years as a gaming destination, "Atlantic City is pushing to reclaim its former status as one of America's top convention destinations" (Nigro, 1998, p. 58).

THE CASE OF PHYSICAL DEVELOPMENT IN OTHER JURISDICTIONS

This paper has focused on casinos and conventions in Las Vegas and Atlantic City. The rationale for this focus is that these two locations are, far and away, the preeminent casino communities in the United States and have the longest history of casino activity. Thus, they are most representative of the relationship between casinos and conventions/meetings. However, during the 1990s, other jurisdictions have legalized gaming, and their relationship with conventions/meetings has paralleled that of the other two.

Physical Development on the Mississippi Gulf Coast

After Las Vegas and Atlantic City, the largest concentration of casinos is along the Mississippi Gulf Coast in the communities of Biloxi and Gulfport, where casino gaming was legalized in 1990. "'Casinos no longer live by gaming alone,' says Tim Hinckley, vice president of marketing for Isle of Capri Casinos" (Plume, 2001, p. 43). Tourism officials are hoping to attract more meetings to the Gulf Coast to counteract the saturation of the gaming market. "This is certainly a market that will continue to increase its attraction to group business" (Nigro, 1998, p. 60).

The Mississippi Coliseum and Convention Center in Biloxi currently has 100,000 square feet of space and is constructing 80,000 more. The center also has a 25,000 square foot arena that can accommodate a maximum of 15,000 people (Ross, 1998). "State tourism officials are in talks with major hotel companies in an effort to get a convention hotel at the coliseum" (Palermo, 2001, p. 17).

Helping to spur development of convention meeting space is state legislation that requires casino operators to reinvest 100% of the value of their casino barges in landside development. The newest casino hotel, Beau Rivage, has 1,780 guest rooms, features a 50,000 square foot convention center, and has a 17,000 square foot ballroom that can accommodate 1,800 conventioneers. The Gulf Resort, opened in 1927, completed a renovation that added 6,000 square feet of meeting space. The Imperial Palace Casino opened a 30,000 square foot convention center that is an addition to the 20,000 square feet of meeting space that existed. The Palace Casino opened in 2000 and includes two multi-function areas at 7,500 and 4,800 square feet, respectively. The Grand Casino in Biloxi expanded in the late 1990s with an additional 500 sleeping rooms, a new 42,000 foot convention center that includes a 17,000 square foot exhibit hall, a 14,000 square foot ballroom, and eight meeting rooms.

Some of the existing hotels also have meeting and convention space. The Isle of Capri, one of the first casinos to open, includes 6,600 feet of meeting space; the President Casino has 50,000 and Treasure Bay has almost 17,000. Additionally, the Grand Casino Biloxi has 42,000 feet of meeting space, while the Grand Casino Gulfport has 12,000.

According to the Harrison County Development Commission, the area hosted 242 meetings and over 80,000 attendees in 1999. This was a 17% increase over the previous year (Ross, 2000). The Mississippi Gulf Coast has followed the lead of other gaming jurisdictions in trying to embrace the meetings and conventions market.

Native American Casinos

Native Americans gained the right to operate casinos in 1987 as a result of a congressional action called the Indian Gaming Regulatory Act. The first casino facility to open was Foxwoods in Connecticut in 1992. It was initially developed with a small 280-room hotel and no meeting space, relying on the casino to attract leisure travelers from the northeast corridor. A museum was added in 1998, and the operators were surprised when it attracted groups and corporations who held meetings there. Today, Foxwoods has over 1,400 rooms with 55,000 square feet of meeting space, including a ballroom with seating for 1,800. "Foxwoods currently hosts 150 to 200 meetings a year, primarily for Northeast based groups" (Harris, 2000, p. 90).

Following the success of Foxwoods, Mohegan Sun opened in the same state in 1996. They, too, had little meeting space when they opened, but are just completing an $800 million expansion that includes 100,000 square feet of meeting space. "'This isn't being built as a hotel with casino attached,' says

David Casey, vice president of sales and marketing. 'It is being built as a meetings and events destination'" (Harris, 2000, p. 90). Other Native American casinos with significant convention/meeting space include Soaring Eagle in Michigan, with 26,000 square feet, and Florida's Miccosukee Resort, with 46,000. The most recent development is the plan by the Seneca Nation to build a new convention center in downtown Buffalo, New York, as part of their casino based entertainment complex.

As can be seen, many Native American gaming venues throughout the United States have developed not only into full scale resorts, but are also focusing on attracting a large number of convention and meeting attendees. They are following the successful strategy of non-Native American casino operators. They are taking advantage of their location by bringing in groups that lack the budget to travel to Las Vegas. Planners are benefiting from this approach with more meeting venues to choose from.

CONCLUSION

Legalized casinos have been operating in the United States for three quarters of a century. For most of that time, casino operators relied almost exclusively on leisure gamblers to generate business. They were too busy operating their casinos for the "core" gambler to notice other opportunities. That changed in the 1980s and 1990s as gaming was legalized in more and more locations, causing concern about competition and saturation. While casinos tried many strategies to broaden their draw beyond the "traditional gambler," the attempts were not as fruitful as they had hoped.

The one strategy that yields success for casino operators around the country is acceptance of the meeting and convention segments. The success of this approach is seen from coast to coast in places like Las Vegas, Atlantic City, Connecticut, and on Native American tribal lands. The strategy works well for a number of reasons. First, casino operators, or more specifically the research analysts at corporate headquarters, determined that convention/meeting attendees could contribute as much as gamblers to the bottom line. This is accomplished through higher room rates, extensive food and beverage or catering revenues, and a longer length of stay, albeit with lower expenditures on the gaming floor. This is in keeping with the new trend toward making the hotel, along with F&B, a profit center. In addition, casino operators determined that high rollers did not want to eat at buffets, but wanted outstanding food and beverage outlets. Since the casinos had already begun adding names like Wolfgang Puck and Emeril to their amenities, this coincided nicely with the needs of conventioneers. Another addition was of retail outlets that are frequented as much by conventioneers as by gamblers. Further, conventioneers prefer to have their events mid-week and non-holiday periods–exactly the opposite of the mainstream gambler. Thus, there is a symbiotic relationship between the casino and convention industries.

The attraction of conventions/meetings to casino destinations is a recent phenomenon that is only now taking hold. Virtually all of the new, billion-dollar resorts being planned in Las Vegas include significant amounts of meeting and convention space. Further, many of the new casino hotels are hiring convention services staff with CIC or MPI certifications, underscoring their commitment to the meetings market. Given the newness of this phenomenon, there is every reason to believe that this trend will continue long into the future.

The reader is reminded that the phenomenon–casinos embracing conventions–is a recent occurrence; therefore, relatively little research has been done in this area. That is why most of the references in this article are from trade articles rather than academic journals–there are virtually no academic articles on this subject. Thus, there is great opportunity for future research. For example, one might try to gather the financial data from hotels regarding spending and occupancy by gamblers versus convention attendees. Analysis could then be undertaken regarding the value of business by segment, market share, and so forth. One could also survey attendees, sponsors, and exhibitors regarding their perception of gaming versus non-gaming destinations. There is much research still to be done.

REFERENCES

Baker, T. (2002, June). New games in town. *Meetings & Conventions, 37*(7), 43-52.

Berns, D. (2001, April). Mandalay Bay: Casino to add convention space. *Las Vegas Review Journal,* 1D.

Bulavsky, J. (1999, June). Upscale shops for thousands of conventioneers. *Casino Journal, XII*(6), 57.

Center for Exhibition Industry Research. (2002). *Exhibition Industry Census.* Chicago: Center for Convention Industry Research.

Cooke, M. (2000, June). New in gaming. *Meetings & Conventions, 36*(7), 51-58.

Finney, M. I. (1997, March). High stakes relationships: Casinos and conventions. *Association Management, 49*(3), 64-66.

Ghitelman, D. (1997, January). The new deal: Will conventions be a player in Atlantic City's future? *Meetings & Conventions, 32*(1), 78-81.

Grimaldi, L. (2000, September). Atlantic City's gamble. *Meetings & Conventions, 35*(7), 87-90.

Hanson, B. (2002, November). Slow to recover, with meetings a priority market. *Convene*, 19-40.

Hardin, T. (2002). It's a push. *Successful Meetings*, 87-93.

Harris, E. (2000, April). Going Native. *Successful Meetings*, 89-91.

Klatzkin, L. (2003). What "Borgata" means. *Global Gaming Business*, 2(10), 10.

McQueen, P. A. (2003, November). Economic climate determining factor in gaming growth. November International Gaming and Wagering Business, *24*: 11, 13, 17.

Macy, R. (2000, February). Casino Executive: Vegas just scratchin' the surface in convention business. Associated Press State and Local Wire: Retrieved October 18, 2002, from *http://web.lexis-nexis.com/doc*

Nigro, D. (1998, June). Betting on meetings. *Meetings & Conventions*, *33*(7), 57-62.

Palermo, D. (2001, May). Southern saturation. *International Gaming and Wagering Business*, 22(5), 13-17.

Palermo, D. (2002, October). Always evolving: The Strip promises to change over the next few years. *International Gaming and Wagering Business*, 23(10), 1-35.

Plume, J. (2001, May). Not by gaming alone. *Casino Journal*, *XIV*(5), 42-44.

Pollock, M. (2003). Rooms to move. *Global Gaming Business*, 2(10, 18-20.

Ross, J. R. (1998, May). Associations betting on attendance appeal of gaming destinations. *Convene, XIII*(4), 81-86.

Ross, J. R. (2000, May). Gaming destination growth remains on upward spiral. *Convene, XV*(4), 73-82.

Shemeligian, B. (1999, July). The new target: To snare the hottest new resort business in Las Vegas, many casinos are building more convention and meeting space. *Casino Journal*, *12*(7)56-58.

Shure, P. (2000, November). Largest shows. *Convene* [Special Issue], 24-27.

Smith, R. (2003, October). Earnings climb for Venetian parent: Convention business helps buoy result analyst says. *Las Vegas Review Journal*. Retrieved on October 30, 2002, from *http://reviewjournal.com/oct-30-wed-2002/business/19951468.html*

Convention Center Wars
and the Decline of Local Democracy

David H. Laslo, PhD
Dennis R. Judd, PhD

SUMMARY. Convention centers have emerged as a focal point in an intense competition among cities for a share of the economically important meetings and exhibition market. In this paper, we present abundant evidence to show that cities can substantially benefit by capturing a share of this market. However, the cost and size of the meetings facilities that are appropriate for particular cities will vary with local circumstances. We argue that such local considerations are ignored because of the political influence that the meetings industry now exerts when cities make decisions about building or expanding convention centers. *[Article copies available for a fee from The Haworth Document Delivery Service: 1-800-HAWORTH. E-mail address: <docdelivery@haworthpress.com> Website: <http://www.HaworthPress.com> © 2004 by The Haworth Press, Inc. All rights reserved.]*

KEYWORDS. Convention centers, meetings, meetings industry, conventions, exhibitions

David H. Laslo is Director MIDAS, Public Policy Research Center, University of Missouri-Saint Louis, 362 SSB, 8001 Natural Bridge Rd., Saint Louis, MO 63121.

Dennis R. Judd is Professor, Department of Political Science and Fellow, Great Cities Institute, University of Illinois at Chicago, 1007 W. Harrison Street, Chicago, IL 60605.

[Haworth co-indexing entry note]: "Convention Center Wars and the Decline of Local Democracy." Laslo, David H., and Dennis R. Judd. Co-published simultaneously in *Journal of Convention & Event Tourism* (The Haworth Hospitality Press, an imprint of The Haworth Press, Inc.) Vol. 6, No. 1/2, 2004, pp. 81-98; and: *Current Issues in Convention and Exhibition Facility Development* (ed: Robert R. Nelson) The Haworth Hospitality Press, an imprint of The Haworth Press, Inc., 2004, pp. 81-98. Single or multiple copies of this article are available for a fee from The Haworth Document Delivery Service [1-800-HAWORTH, 9:00 a.m. - 5:00 p.m. (EST). E-mail address: docdelivery@haworthpress.com].

http://www.haworthpress.com/web/JCET
© 2004 by The Haworth Press, Inc. All rights reserved.
Digital Object Identifier: 10.1300/J452v06n01_06

Convention centers have emerged as a focal point in the intense competition among cities for a share of the economically vital meetings and exhibition market. Although the unremitting push for additional space and amenities has sparked local debates about public costs and benefits, larger and larger centers have continued to be built at a furious pace. In the decade between 1992 and 2002, existing convention centers increased total exhibition space by 16 million square feet, to 72.4 million square feet, and 14 new facilities were opened in the year between August 2001 and July 2002 (Andrews, 2002). Once sponsored by civic efforts and financed mainly with private dollars, convention centers have become products of an alliance between local advocates for convention centers and the professionals, associations, publications, and consultants that make up a highly complex convention and meetings industry. As a consequence, convention center politics has been moved from the arena of democratic institutions and public debate into a closed policy system dominated by professionals and specialists who share an interest in promoting the construction and expansion of convention centers, irrespective of local needs.

Conventions and meetings are but two components of a vast tourism/entertainment sector[1] that has helped to revitalize local economies in recent decades. Cities have devoted huge resources to developing tourism/entertainment as a vital component of local economies. Driven by the pressures of fiscal stress and the dynamics of inter-urban competition, cities have committed billions of public dollars since the 1970s to an impressive array of new facilities: convention centers, convention-center headquarters hotels, festival malls and retail malls, waterfront developments, sports stadiums and arenas, museums, urban entertainment districts, and (in a few cities) gaming casinos (Judd, 2003). In the United States, more than $2 billion was spent annually in the early 1990s on sports facilities and convention centers alone (Eisinger, 2000). The race to build facilities shows no sign of slowing down; convention centers keep expanding, stadiums become larger and more expensive, and the variety and complexity of entertainment venues keeps increasing (Judd, 2003).

The physical reconstruction of cities was made possible by a comprehensive restructuring of local public institutions and processes. Confronted by the fact that city government was too bureaucratic and fiscally limited to undertake expensive new projects, in the 1980s, energetic mayors and other civic leaders pioneered in the development of new institutions that could accomplish public purposes but not be bound by the rules that frustrated general-purpose governments. These public/private authorities were able to operate much like private corporations, thereby avoiding public scrutiny of their operations (Perry, 2003). Equally important, they were often empowered to borrow money, issue bonds, and exercise critical powers such as eminent domain. These institutional arrangements are the key to understanding how fiscally strapped cities were able to build the facilities and undertake the ambitious projects necessary to support a local economy of tourism and entertainment.

Public officials and the proponents of new facilities became adept at bypassing the public (Eisinger, 2000). Referenda on major capital projects were once the norm, but they had become increasingly rare by the 1990s. Where it was still necessary to ask voters to approve tax increases or bond issues for new facilities, a formidable coalition could be assembled to push for the new projects. In the case of convention centers, a constellation of specialists from the convention and meetings industry became adroit at working with local allies to promote the construction and expansion of meetings facilities.

However much this arrangement may have contributed to the extraordinary pace of convention center construction and expansion in recent decades, it is important to acknowledge that in recent years, conventions, meetings, and business travel have been essential for local economic vitality and the revitalization of downtowns. In the first sections of this paper, we offer compelling evidence on this point in order to emphasize that our critical perspective on convention center politics is not built upon any doubts about the importance of conventions and meetings to urban economies.

For us, the question is not whether cities should invest in convention centers, convention center hotels, or other accoutrements of a tourism infrastructure. The issue is whether the decisions made about these investments involve a full range of participants and the possibility of vigorous public debate. In a political and economic environment in which political power is generally fragmented and diffused within municipalities, policy entrepreneurs are tempted to find ways around democratic processes. We argue that the proponents of convention centers have largely bypassed local democratic processes, with the result that new facilities and expansions have often been undertaken irrespective of whether they will enhance the ability of a particular city to successfully compete for a larger share of conventions and meetings.[2] As a means of illustrating how this politics unfolds, we present a brief case study of convention center politics in St. Louis, Missouri. The St. Louis case demonstrates that decisions about the city's investment in its convention center have been made within a closed community linking local proponents with the meetings industry. At the conclusion to the paper, we provide evidence that the St. Louis case is not exceptional but typical of most cities in the United States, and perhaps elsewhere.

COMPETING FOR TOURISM

The mass tourism that has become so familiar today is a recent phenomenon that was spawned by a growing middle class that emerged in the United

States and Europe after the Second World War (Jackle, 1985). With post-war affluence and the development of integrated transportation systems, within three decades, business trips and family vacations became the norm for white-collar workers and middle-class families in the developed world. In the 1980s, growing prosperity in Asia and other regions of the world made tourism a truly global phenomenon. The decades-long growth and the globalization of business travel and leisure travel has made the travel and tourism industry into a powerful generator of jobs and profits. According to the Travel Industry Association of America (TIA), by 1998, the tourism industry was the largest services export industry in the United States (Travel Industry Association of America (TIA), 1998). Travel-related spending in the United States shot up by 95% between 1986 and 1996, but over the same period, travel spending by international visitors rose by 246% (World Tourism Organization (WTO), 1997). In the U.S., tourist receipts (adjusted in 1984 dollars) increased from $26 billion in 1986 to $90 billion in 1996 (WTO, 1997). The U.S. remains among the top three destinations in the world, behind France and Spain (WTO, 1999).

With its ability to generate local revenue streams through a variety of ad valorem and use taxes and its ability to generate jobs, there are ample justifications for investing in tourism. When taking into account the $446 billion spent on domestic travel and $75 billion spent by international travelers in the United States in 1998, if a city captured even a very modest market share, it would have generated badly needed revenue and employment (Office of Travel and Tourism Institute, 1999). The 1.2 billion total person trips in the United States in 1998 resulted in 6.8 million jobs and generated $67 billion in federal, state and local taxes (TIA, 1998).

Visitors pay higher taxes and some that local residents do not. According to the Travel Industry Association of America (TIA) in 1998, governmental jurisdictions derive revenue from travel and tourism components such as airline arrivals, airport facility charges, gasoline, restaurants, hotels, auto rentals, and user fees (TIA, 1998). As an example of the magnitude of the revenue potential, U.S. hotel and motel revenue was estimated to be $84 billion in 2000, roughly 28% of total world accommodation revenue. Using the national average hotel tax rate of 12%, this represented approximately $10 billion in tax revenue to be spread around the nation's cities (TIA, 1998).

In addition, the facilities devoted to tourism and entertainment have become essential to the revitalization of central cities. A recent national survey confirms that cities all over the United States, of all sizes and within and outside of metropolitan areas, have built the physical infrastructure of tourism/entertainment. Sixty-three percent of the central cities (cities of 50,000 or more) had built or were planning to build convention centers; two-thirds had undertaken to build sports stadiums, 65% had built or were developing a festival-retail mall, and much most of them had developed a cultural district, entertainment-restaurant district, framer's market, performing arts center, and a historic district or site (Judd, Winter, Barnes, & Stern, 2003). The amenities of tourism/entertainment have become essential components in the rebound of downtowns. The highly paid professionals that have led the recent revival place a high premium on the mix of amenities and activities that add up to an exciting street life and lifestyle. In sum, the new infrastructure and amenities of tourism and entertainment offer far more benefit to cities than the attraction of out-of-town visitors.

THE MEETINGS INDUSTRY

The meetings industry, which includes exhibitions, trade shows, consumer shows and association and corporate meetings, has been expanding rapidly in recent years, and it is likely to continue to do so. The new "lean and mean" and flexible corporate structure, based on horizontal rather than vertical organization, relies heavily on meetings. Furthermore, the increased specialization that has occurred in almost every profession has caused specialists to seek out kindred types in other locales across the world when the number of "niche" specialists (for example, thorax surgeons, scholars of urban politics) at any given local is generally very small (Shure, 1996a). Also contributing to the continued use of meetings is the preference of an ever-increasing number of women in the labor force, who prefer meetings, conventions, and trade shows to other types of business travel (62.4% to 42.4% for men) (Successful Meetings, 1996).

Communications and information technology has increased the number of contacts that can be made and serves to remind people of their need to make personal contact, to press the flesh (Shure, 1996b). The new technology has likewise increased the efficiency and productivity of meetings, making one of the primary tasks of associations (the continued education of its membership) easier. In a 1997 survey of 5,500 national associations, the American Society of Association Executives found that seven out of ten Americans belonged to at least one association and that one out of four belonged to four or more (Hedelad, 1998). The attraction of membership in business, professional, or service associations appears to be increasing because it is the primary source of adult continuing education and a source for networking in a highly mobile labor market.

The number of business- and professional-related meetings held each year is huge. In 2002, there were nearly 23,000 associations and 6.5 million total private business establishments (with 143,000 establishments of 100 employees or more) in the United States (Hedelad, 2002; U.S. Dept. of Commerce, 1994). Businesses hold many off-premises meetings a year that require significant space. It is a fair assumption that every professional association has at least one major meeting annually, and some number of more specialized or regional meetings, to educate its membership about the latest industry innovations and information. According to a meetings industry survey published in 1996, the typical association holds a mean of 2.8 events with exhibitions each year, and over a third of these groups (34.6%) have budgets of over $1 million (Shure, 1996a). In addition, there were 9,370 trade shows held in North America in 1997, with 375 of those never having been held before (Directory of Trade Shows, 1997).

There is a growing number of tourism and meetings-related associations, and their membership and number of professional employees have also increased. Before 1960, there were 29 associations representing the hospitality, travel, and exhibition and meeting planner professions. By 2001, those numbers had grown to 154 associations with a membership of over 1.5 million (Hedelad, 2002). With the number, size, and variety of meetings on a continual upward trajectory, new professions and occupations have emerged to accommodate the needs of companies and nonprofit organizations and associations. Professional meeting planners have emerged as important actors in the industry. They now plan about two-thirds of all meetings held by corporations and associations, and about 20% of those meetings are organized by professionals who are working independently of the organization sponsoring the event (Successful Meetings, 2001).

As the number, size, and variety of meetings have grown, so has the industry's contribution to the national economy. In a study sponsored by the Convention Liaison Council in 1994, the meetings industry employed more than 1.5 million persons full-time while generating $82.8 billion in direct spending, which amounted to approximately 2% of Gross National Product (Tanner, 1997). This spending translated into $12.3 billion in tax revenues, with nearly $2 billion (15.6%) of this amount going to local governments. To put this into perspective, this was a little less than half of the annual appropriation for the Community Development Block Grant Program ($4.675 billion in 1998), which has been a staple of central-city governments since the 1970s.

Besides the obvious attraction to local governments, a variety of local actors have more than a passing interest in the revenue and profit potential from conventions and meetings. As shown in Table 1, the meetings industry contributed over a third of hotel revenues in 1994 while supplying almost a fifth of all airline revenues. Meetings and trade-show spending also accounted for more than 10% of restaurant and business services, 9% of ground transporta-

TABLE 1. Industry Recipients of Meetings and Trade Show Spending

	Direct Spending (In Millions)	Percent of Total
Hotel and Other Meeting Places	$18.40	35.2
Air Transportation	$10.01	19.2
Restaurants	$5.65	10.8
Business Services	$5.49	10.5
Ground Transportation	$4.70	9.0
Retail Trade	$3.61	6.9
Entertainment	$1.25	2.4
Advertising	$0.21	0.4
Equipment Rentals	$0.52	1.0
Misc./Other Business Expenses	$2.40	4.6
Total	$52.27	100.0

Source: Tanner, 1997.

tion, and nearly 7% of retail trade. These averages vastly underestimate the heavy reliance of businesses in central business districts and other areas with a concentration of meetings facilities. The larger meetings, such as exhibitions, trade shows, and conventions, contributed 25.2%, or $16.6 billion, in hotel revenues and 11.5%, or $10 billion, in airline revenues, a remarkably significant proportion of all revenues in these industries. Obviously, there are likely to be an impressive number of avid supporters for most convention-center projects.

THE EXHIBITION, TRADE SHOW, AND CONVENTION INDUSTRIES

The exhibitions (or expositions, as they are sometimes called) segment of the U.S. meetings industry began in the United States when the first exhibition was held at the newly constructed Chicago Interstate Industrial Exposition Building in 1873 (Tanner, 1997). Largely confined to local or regional shows until the post-World War II period, after the war the number of exhibitions grew quickly in step with the surge in pent-up demand for mass-produced consumer goods, increasingly efficient national distribution of products and services, and widespread domestic air travel. It soon became clear that exhibitions could become more than a sales "contact and close" medium, but also an integral part of marketing and advertising. The invention of Masonite, spray paint, and lacquer made it possible for sign shops to create new and improved marketing accoutrements for exhibition booths, thus spawning another exhibition-related industry (Tanner, 1997).

Even the economic contraction of the 1970s stimulated the exhibitions market by exerting pressure to maximize the marketing dollar. Exhibitions took on greater significance because of the number of contacts and leads that could be developed within the confines of an exhibition hall. It was estimated in 1996 that it cost nearly twice as much for a field sales call ($997) as it did to close an exhibition lead ($550) (Tanner, 1997). The Center for Exhibition Research Center (CEIR) estimates that between 1989 and 1997, 1,047 new exhibition shows were held with a total increase in attendance of 50 million people. This translated into an increase of 83%, an average 9.2% per year (Tanner, 1997).

Obviously, the meetings and exhibition industry is a major contributor to the economic vitality of the national and state and local economies and also serves as a vehicle for marketing efforts, adult education, and the dissemination of industry and professional information. Given the magnitude of the spending that this industry generates, it is not surprising that the number of convention facilities and the amount of exhibition space continues to grow. For convention center proponents, the justification of gaining even a fraction of a percent of this huge market is enough to mobilize the necessary local and non-local resources to build and expand facilities.

THE GROWTH OF FACILITIES AND EXHIBITION SPACE

Once the construction of a tourism and meetings infrastructure was recognized as a viable alternative to the indiscriminate "smokestack chasing" of the 1970s and early 1980s (Eisinger, 1988), cities engaged in a virtual arms race to build convention centers. By the 1990s, most cities had replaced their Depression-era auditoriums with facilities that had all the accoutrements of a contemporary meeting and exhibition facility, such as large exhibition halls, multiple loading docks, conference centers, ballrooms and spacious lobbies that allowed plenty of room for registration and multiple events. The demands for larger exhibition spaces with a full range of technological features have continued to push cities and their proponents to seek bigger and better facilities (Shure, 2000).

In spite of the economic downturn and the impact of the events of September 11, 2001, industry sources predicted that an expected recovery by late 2003 or 2004 would stimulate a pent-up demand for exhibition space that would be met by an ample supply of new centers and expanded space in existing facilities

(Andrews, 2002). According to the *Major Exhibition Hall Directory* for 2002, in just 4 years, from 1998 to 2002, the amount of space increased by 9.4 million square feet, with 30 facilities offering more than 500,000 square feet of exhibition space. Nearly half (195) of the 415 facilities in North America surveyed by *Tradeshow Weekly* offered between 100,000 and 499,999 square feet of exhibition space (Andrews, 2002). Fourteen new facilities were opened between August 2001 and July 2002, which produced an additional 3.3 million square feet. A total of 87 new and expanded facilities were slated to offer 12.2 million square feet of new exhibition space beginning in the second half of 2002, and by the end of the decade another 3.2 million square feet, to be built at the cost of over $7 billion, was in the planning stages (Andrews, 2002). Although a 3.1% decline in the size of exhibitions and shows caused some concern about overbuilding, the convention center wars showed no signs of abating.

Data based on information supplied by the individual convention and visitors bureaus (CVBs) of cities in the United States shows that in the decades since World War II, virtually all cities with a population of more than 100,000 built convention centers and that many smaller cities did so as well. Table 2 shows the number of facilities built in each decade from before the 1930s through 1998 (note that these data do not include expansions). Before 1930, there were 19 facilities in the country, and only 14 more were added in the next two decades. In the 1950s, 25 more came on line. The proliferation of convention and exhibition facilities began in earnest in the 1960s and accelerated in the 1970s and 1980s as air travel, rising affluence, and greater specialization in the job market gave rise to more meetings with exhibitions, consumer shows (such as autos, boats, and electronics), and conventions (Jewell, 1992; Tanner, 1997, pp. 8-9). Nearly a quarter of all exhibition facilities currently in use by 1998 were built in the 1970s, and 7 out of 10 (or 70.6%) were built after 1970. The volume of exhibition space likewise expanded, with over three-quarters (75.7%) of new exhibition space available in the United States in 1998 built since the 1960s. Over the same period, the space added through expansions could conservatively be estimated to be another two to three million square feet.

By any measure, the growth in the number of facilities and square feet of exhibition space since the 1970s is nothing short of spectacular. In light of the potential benefits for cities, it is not hard to explain all this activity. However, cities differ significantly from one another. For some, it may be wise to limit their participation in the convention wars to well-designed, smaller facilities targeted at smaller meetings and exhibitions. In fact, however, the evaluation about what is appropriate and realistic for a particular city is rarely, if ever, conducted by local participants. Instead, the professionals in the industry supply the data, do the studies, and often help manage the public relations effort. The result is that the size and the cost of meetings facilities are not correlated

TABLE 2. Summary of Exhibition Facilities by Year of Opening*

	Cities 100,000+		Cities < 100,000		Total All Cities	
	Number of Exhibition		Number of Exhibition		Number of Exhibition	
	Facilities	Space	Facilities	Space	Facilities	Space
Pre-1930s	17	2,840,189	2	458,600	19	3,298,789
1930s	4	701,800	3	156,000	7	857,800
1940s	5	428,597	2	350,000	7	778,597
1950s	17	4,178,162	8	4,340,253	25	8,518,415
1960s	45	10,210,910	17	1,123,710	62	11,334,620
1970s	54	8,096,321	42	2,900,369	96	10,996,690
1980s	64	9,535,049	40	1,694,584	104	11,229,633
1990-1998	42	5,221,124	47	2,960,045	89	8,181,169
Total	248	41,212,152	161	13,983,561	409	55,195,713

*Includes convention centers, arenas, pavilions, coliseums, and auditoriums that promote space for exhibitions. Does not include outdoor facilities. Of 544 facilities identified, 409 opening dates have been verified as of 1998.
Source: Meeting planner's guides for respective cities; Welch, 1998; and Meetings Industry Mall Venue Database, 1998.

closely with the size, geographic location, and economic condition of the cities that build them. A brief history of convention center politics in St. Louis reveals that this occurs because specialists within the industry exert an overwhelming influence over the decisions that cities make about convention centers.

ST. LOUIS AND THE CONVENTION CENTER WARS

In the post-World War II period, St. Louis's politics was substantially defined by a powerful civic leadership that worked closely with activist mayors to define the local public agenda. The foundation of this political structure was laid in 1952 when Mayor Joseph M. Darst convened a group of civic leaders in his office and asked them to take a leading role in the city's urban renewal program. Subsequently, 65 business leaders raised $2 million in capital for the new urban redevelopment corporation, which also served as the conduit for federal urban renewal funds (Institute of Housing, 1952). In 1953, again with the urging of Mayor Darst, a group of eight corporate executives agreed to serve as the board members of a new civic organization, Civic Progress, Inc., a group that represented only the largest corporations in the city (the board would grow to as many as 31 members by 1966) (Sanford, 1996). Working closely with activist mayors, Civic Progress formed an urban regime[3] capable of pushing forward an agenda for the revitalization of the downtown. For example, in cooperation with the Chamber of Commerce of Metropolitan St. Louis, Civic Progress took the lead in the development of a new baseball stadium to house the Cardinals baseball team. By 1961, civic leaders had raised $20 million in private capital pledges for the stadium. With a tax referendum carefully orchestrated by the Chamber and Civic Progress (passed on the second try), enough public and private money was raised to build the stadium, which opened in 1965.

Civic Progress was also a key driving force behind the development of St. Louis's first convention center. When the $36 million, 240,000 square feet Cervantes Convention Center opened in March 1977, it was viewed as both an essential tax-generating project that could prop up a sagging local treasury and as a vehicle for downtown revitalization. With its tax base shrinking due to rapid population decentralization and loss of manufacturing jobs in automobiles and steel, civic leaders saw options for revitalizing their downtown. Editorials of the day featured tag lines like "Thanks to Convention Center Color Tourism Picture Green" and "Our Community's Hopes are Rising with the Convention Center." The Cervantes Convention Center was St. Louis' first entry into the emerging meetings and exhibition sweepstakes and was reported to be the ninth largest in the United States (Jones, 1977).

Located on the northern end of a desolate and bleak downtown, the new center featured a box design that included some convention center bare essentials–three meeting halls, a lobby, loading docks, and kitchen facilities. The "box with docks," as it came to be called, was noteworthy for its poor design and rapid descent into near obsolescence within 5 years of its opening. Almost immediately the center's sound system needed replacement and the roof suffered from damaging leaks. The center's dock design limited the ability to hold overlapping events, and its austere façade gave it an uninviting appearance (Faust, 1997). In less than a year, the city sold additional bonds as part of a refinancing effort and in response to revenue shortfalls and "no-show" conventions, cancelled because of an inadequate number of hotel rooms. After the refinancing, about $6 million became available for repairs and improvements (Meyer, 1979)

But to the convention center staff, such modest steps were not nearly enough. The center's director brought the city's budget director on board behind an effort to persuade civic leaders that a major expansion was needed. Together they convinced the mayor and the board of aldermen to finance an initial feasibility study. In its 1984 report, Laventhol and Horwath, a national public accounting firm with a convention center division, told the city that expansion would be necessary to keep the city competitive in the meetings and exhibition market. Citing industry data on convention center space, tax rates, and economic multipliers, Laventhol and Horwath concluded that without the proposed expansion, the city would rank 25th in the nation, but with the expansion, it would move up to eighth (Laventhol & Horwath, 1984). But by 2002, in spite of the expansion, St. Louis' 502,000 square feet of exhibition space ranked 24th in the United States (Andrews, 2002).

Subsequent studies by Lavanthol and Horwath and by Public Finance Management of Memphis, Tennessee, provided a blueprint for financing the expansion. Included in these studies were analyses of the economic impact of potential market shares that had been supplied by industry associations such as CEIR and *Tradeshow Weekly*. In February 1991, another study conducted by one of the Big Eight public accounting firms, Coopers & Lybrand, provided economic impact and market share analyses (including generic "multiplier" estimates of local economic impact derived from studies conducted for other cities) (Coopers & Lybrand, 1991). Still another study in April 1991 by KMPG (Peat Marwick) provided similar analyses for a combined convention center expansion and domed stadium (KMPG (Peat Marwick), 1991).

National architectural firms submitted competing bids for the design of the expansion and remake of the existing center. A local but internationally prominent firm, Hellmuth, Obata & Kassenbaum (HOK), was selected after what local observers called a "stupendous" presentation. It selected a local engineering firm, Campbell Design, to provide engineering services. However, top-level development officials sought and hired a Chicago architectural firm, Skidmore, Owings & Merrill (SOM) to re-evaluate the HOK design in the late 1980s, which resulted in design changes and added amenities as well as tens of millions in additional cost. The cost of the redesign work alone exceeded $5 million.

It Is Important To Note That, In A Sharp Departure From The Past, Civic Progress Did Not Set The Agenda By Proposing The Expansion, And They Were Not Involved In Any Of The Project's Details. They Played A Passive–Even Reactive– Role. The Campaign To Persuade Voters To Approve An Increase In Hotel And Restaurant Taxes To Finance The Expansion Was Run By The Local Office Of An International Public Relations Firm, Fleischmann- Hilliard, With Financial Contributions from Civic Progress. After some hesitation, local hotel and restaurant associations endorsed the project and the tax referendum passed by a razor-thin margin of 337 votes, with a 22% turnout (O'Neil, 1987).

The politics surrounding the expansion proposal revealed that Civic Progress had withdrawn from its activist leadership role in St. Louis.[4] Symptomatic of the new behind-the-scenes leadership style was the protocol that was to be observed when trying to access Civic Progress and its members. Beginning in the late 1970s, public policy proposals being considered by Civic Progress were first presented to a representative of Fleischmann-Hilliard, which had a sizable St. Louis office. The Fleischmann-Hilliard representative would then decide the merits of proposals before presenting a short list to Civic Progress. This vetting process allowed corporate leaders to pick and choose among ideas and projects without the possibility of public disclosure.

The new procedure revealed a fundamental restructuring of local politics in which civic leadership was being replaced by policy professionals (Laslo, 2003). In the past, Civic Progress had been instrumental in setting the local agenda and working out the details of proposals, including financing and political strategy. These steps were now being taken over by professional specialists, who then tried to enlist support and assistance from corporate leaders. Even in the referendum campaigns, data was supplied and public relations were managed by local and non-local professionals in the meetings industry. The series of consulting reports provided economic and fiscal justifications for the expansion of the Cervantes Center and a blueprint for its financing. Local institutions such as the St. Louis Convention and Visitors Bureau provided marketing expertise and individual members of its board lent their voices to the arguments for the expansion. Civic Progress supplied some funds, but its members remained mostly silent.

After 9 years of political maneuvering, planning, and construction, the expansion opened on May 7, 1993, to great expectations and self-congratulations. Over the course of 3 days of events, convention and development officials were praised for producing a design that was aesthetically pleasing and that possessed all the requisite amenities and functions of a contemporary exhibition and meeting facility. A redesign of the docks, the addition of a 1,400-seat lecture hall, and the "largest ballroom west of the Mississippi," all combined to produce an outstanding facility. Two years later, a multi-purpose domed stadium attached to the convention center was completed (the Trans World Dome; renamed the Edward D. Jones Dome in 1992). When not used for sporting or other events, the domed stadium can be opened to the convention center for an additional 162,000 square feet of exhibition space, which is essential for large events such as auto and home and garden shows.

Considered to be a model for multi-purpose facilities, the $260 million, 340,000 square foot expansion and the $260 million, 62,000-seat domed stadium received high marks from the industry for its functionality and design. Together, the center and the stadium employed several hundred workers on an operating budget of just over $30 million in 2001 (St. Louis Convention and Visitors Commission, 2001). Like convention centers elsewhere, the center continued to need public subsidies to meet operations expenditures, in this case because construction costs dramatically exceeded earlier estimates.

Drawing upon the feedback from meeting planners and exhibition show promoters and their needs, local managers had made a series of design changes that increased the cost of the expansion from an original $60 million to $160 million when it was completed (Laslo, Louishomme, Phares, & Judd, 2003). The multi-purpose structure now needed approximately $2 million per year in subsidies from the city in order to meet its budget (St. Louis Convention and Visitors Commission, 2001).

THE ST. LOUIS CASE IS NOT EXCEPTIONAL

The St. Louis case is not exceptional. As more and more cities have entered the convention center sweepstakes, it has become abundantly clear that the decisions about constructing and expanding convention facilities bypass local political processes in key respects. Local advocates call upon industry sources for a ready supply of expertise and information. Consultants' studies are the necessary prelude to bond issuances and tax referenda (where these are necessary). Consulting reports establish an asymmetry of information that gives proponents a monopoly over information so that opponents appear to be uninformed and biased. More generally, the reports also form the basis of a standard narrative of urban decline and growth that ties the construction or expansion of a convention facility to the future prospects and the image of the city.

Because a broad array of consultants and industry specialists provide all relevant financial, public relations, marketing, and expertise to all cities, the same political process is replicated over and over and from place to place (Sanders, 1992). Engineering and architectural services are frequently offered by a handful of national firms. National public relations firms also are regularly hired to manage promotional campaigns, often from concept to tax approval campaign to construction. Likewise, national public accounting and public finance consulting firms with specialties in project finance and cost-benefit analysis provide the principal justifications for individual projects, and they justify public subsidies through feasibility and impact analyses (Sanders, 1999). At the heart of these reports are data and information gathered from industry associations and publications. In turn, accounting and bond-rating firms rely on the same sources of data and on consulting reports from the same firms retained by cities.

After the initial round of facility development in the 1970s and 1980s, when most cities replaced their Depression-era auditoriums and coliseums with contemporary convention centers, subsequent facilities and expansions have been as much a product of replication as local initiative. In most cases, consultants' studies utilize methods of analysis that are, in effect, pre-packaged templates applied across all cities. The standard narrative justifying construction and expansion refers to rankings of a city's convention center size, which provides an automatic justification for expansion. There are also references to the potential economic and tax revenue windfalls that may be gained by capturing a larger share of the market and to the missed opportunities for cities that fail to compete. In the skillful hands of major public relations firms, a taut "sink or swim" story unfolds.

The boilerplate nature of these studies ought to provoke some skepticism. Projections and estimates of economic impact generally utilize dubious multipliers that are applied uniformly across all cities. A recent analysis of these types of studies in 22 cities, including Anaheim, Atlanta, Boston, Denver, Los Angeles, Philadelphia, and Washington, D.C., have shown that projected tax revenues and economic development generally have not materialized (Sanders, 1999). The reason for the disappointing record is not difficult to identify: forecasts of demand have not matched performance because "consultants have made use of essentially the same [nationally derived] data" for every city that retains them (Sanders, 1999). Ignoring local variations certainly makes the consultants' job easier, but it does not give individual cities the nuanced information they require for making judicious decisions about how much to invest in their convention facilities.

Convention centers may impose costs as well as benefits to a city. New space for meetings and exhibitions has far outpaced market demand (Perry, 2003). Only a handful of centers in prime destinations operate at a profit, which leaves calculations of benefit to doubtful multipliers (Shure, 1994). Industry analysts are likely to look at such considerations differently than cities do. For meeting planners and the groups they work for, more space for meetings and conventions is an unalloyed benefit; it expands their options and strengthens their bargaining power with convention center administrators. Those who advise cities to build and expand their facilities do not share in the costs or the risks assumed by local taxpayers.

There are ample reasons why cities would want to enter the meetings and exhibitions sweepstakes, and probably all cities that do so benefit in some way–often substantially. But the terms of the competition must be carefully assessed; otherwise, it is certain that some cities will spend more public money than is justified. Already in a chronic fiscal bind, some cities may find themselves worse off than before, especially if they have foreclosed other possible public ventures with a huge commitment to a newer and bigger convention center. One size does not fit all. But in the virtual war raging among cities for a share of the meetings pie, cities are rarely in a position to make their own assessment. The one certainty is that the experts to whom they turn to for advice always think that more is magnificent and bigger is better.

NOTES

1. For purposes of syntax and brevity, we refer to this sector as the tourist/entertainment sector. It is composed, however, of a complex mixture of activities that may variously (and often loosely) be labeled tourism, leisure, entertainment, and culture. The World Tourism Organization defines a tourist as a traveler who stays overnight (World Tourism Organization, 1995). By employing the concept of entertainment in tandem with tourism, we are intending to recognize that the facilities and events included within the language of "tourism/entertainment" are used and attended by local residents, visitors from the wider region, and officially-defined tourists.

2. For a broader analysis that encompasses other facilities of the tourism/entertainment infrastructure in cities, see Dennis R. Judd and Dick Simpson, "Tourism and the New Urban Politics: The Role of External Constituencies in Building Urban Tourism," *American Behavioral Scientist*, April 2003, Volume 46, Number 8.

3. The concept of urban regimes is based on the recognition that local politics involves more than what government does; it involves the coordination of public power and private resources. Public officials possess crucial resources to guide urban development, but business institutions control access to investment and jobs; thus, these two groups need one another. As political scientist Clarence Stone noted about politics in Atlanta, "What makes governance in Atlanta effective is not the formal machinery of government but rather the informal partnership between city hall and the downtown business elite. This informal partnership and the way it operates constitutes the city's regime; it is the same means through which major policy decisions are made" (Stone, 1989, p. 3). In Stone's account, the "regime" in Atlanta has involved a long-time, continuing, cooperative relationship between a succession of mayors and the city's business elite.

4. The construction of other facilities connected to the tourism/entertainment infrastructure in St. Louis–three sports facilities, two downtown malls, and a casino–show the same pattern (Laslo, Louishomme, Phares, & Judd, 2003).

REFERENCES

Andrews, C. (Ed.). (2002, August). *Major Exhibit Hall Directory* (25th ed.). Secaucus, NJ: Reed Business Information, Inc.

Coopers & Lybrand. (1991, February 27). *Analysis of net fiscal benefit generated from the construction and operation of the expanded Cervantes Convention Center.* Dallas, TX: Author.

Directory of Trade Shows. (1997). *Trade Show Central.* Retrieved May 20, 1998, from *www.tsnn.com*

Eisenger, P. (2000, January). The politics of bread and circuses. *Urban Affairs Review*, *35*(3), 316-333.

Eisinger, P. K. (1988). *The rise of the entrepreneurial state: State and local economic development policy in the United States.* Madison: University of Wisconsin Press.

Faust, F. (1997, September 27). From "Box with Docks" to plush hall. *Saint Louis Post Dispatch*, pp. E1, E7.

Hedelad, A. (Ed.). (1998). *Encyclopedia of Associations* (34th ed., Vol. 1, Parts 1 & 2). Foster, CA: Gale Group.

Hedelad, A. (Ed.). (2002). *Encyclopedia of Associations* (38th ed., Vol. 1, Parts 1 & 2). Foster, CA: Gale Group.

Institute of Housing. (1952, March 21-22). "Proceedings." St. Louis: University College, Washington University.

Iommazzo, A. (Ed.). (2001, January). *State of the industry 2001: Meetings snapshot.* New York: BILL Communications, Inc.

Jackle, J. A. (1985). *The tourist: Travel in the twentieth century North America.* Lincoln: University of Nebraska Press.

Jewell, D. (1992). *Public Assembly Facilities* (2nd ed.). Malabar, FL: Krieger Publishing Co.

Jones, L. L. (1977, March 30). Gateway Center dream in 1968, now a reality. *Saint Louis Post Dispatch*, p. 1B.

Judd, D. R. (Ed.). (2003). *The infrastructure of play: Building the tourist city.* Armonk, NY: M.E. Sharpe.

Judd, D. R., & Simpson, D. (2003, April). Tourism and the new urban politics: The role of external constituencies in building urban tourism. *American Behavioral Scientist, 46*(8), 1056-1069.

Judd, D. R., Winter, W. R., Barnes, W. R., & Stern, E. (2003). Tourism and entertainment as local economic development: A national survey. In D. R. Judd (Ed.), *The infrastructure of play: Building the tourist city* (pp. 50-76). Armonk, NY: M.E. Sharpe.

KPMG (Peat Marwick). (1991, April). *Cervantes Convention and Stadium Complex financial analysis.* Tampa, FL: Author.

Laslo, D. (2003, April). Policy communities and the infrastructure of urban tourism. *American Behavioral Scientist,* 1078-1080.

Laslo, D., Louishomme, C., Phares, D., & Judd, D. (2003). Building the infrastructure of urban tourism: The case of St. Louis. In D. R. Judd (Ed.), *The infrastructure of play: Building the tourist city* (pp. 77-103). Armonk, NY: M.E. Sharpe.

Laventhol & Horwath. (1984). *Market Analysis of the Saint Louis Cervantes Convention Center.* New York: Author.

Meetings Industry Mall Venue Database. (1998). Retrieved July 1998 from *http://www.mim.com/cgibin/var/cardinal/home_count.html*

Meyer, P. (1979, March 15). "No show" conventions are costly. *Saint Louis Post Dispatch*, p. 1E.

Office of Travel and Tourism Institute. (1999). Dept. of Commerce. Retrieved January 10, 1999, from *www.tinet.ita.doc.gov*

O'Neil, T. (1987, November 4). City voters approve Cervantes measures. *Saint Louis Post Dispatch*, pp. 1A, 9A.

Perry, D. (2003). Urban tourism and the privatizing discourses of public infrastructure. In D. R. Judd (Ed.), *The infrastructure of play: Building the tourist city* (pp. 23-70). Armonk, NY: M.E. Sharpe.

St. Louis Convention and Visitors Commission. (2001). Combined statement of revenues and expenditures and changes in fund balance. In *Independent auditor's report* (p. 3). St. Louis, MO.

Sanders, H. T. (1992). Building the convention city: Politics, finance and public investment in urban America. *Journal of Urban Affairs, 14*(2), 135-159.

Sanders, H. T. (1999). Flawed forecasts: A critical look at convention center feasibility studies. White Paper No. 9. Pioneer Institute.

Sanford, R. K. (1996, October 30). Civic Progress, Inc., members contribute in team pattern. *St. Louis Post Dispatch*, p. 1A, 10A.

Shure, P. (1994, May). A bold prediction of the privatization of bureaus. *Convene*, 51.

Shure, P. (1996a, March). The future of meetings. *Convene, XI*(2), 34-50.

Shure, P. (1996b, March). Our increasing reliance on technology will remind us what being human is all about. *Convene, XI*(2), 61.

Shure, P. (2000, October). Sustaining the "Golden Age." *Convene, XV*(2), 4.

Stone, C. (1989). *Regime politics: Governing Atlanta 1946-1988*. Lawrence: University of Kansas Press.

Tanner, J. H., Jr. (1997). *1997 Guide to Exhibition Marketing and Management* (2nd ed.). Bethesda, MD: Center for Exhibition Research.

Travel Industry Association of America (TIA). (1998). *The Travel and Tourism Industry Outlook For 1998*. Washington, D.C.: Travel Industry Association of America.

U.S. Dept of Commerce. (1996, March 15). *County Business Patterns, United States 1994-97*. Retrieved December 15, 1998, from *http://censtats.census.gov/ncbpsic/cbpsic.shtml*

Welch, A. (Ed.). (1996, July). *State of the industry 1996*. New York: BILL Communications, Inc.

Welch, A. (Ed.). (1998, March 31). *SourceBook: 1998 international guide–Meeting facilities and destinations* (Vol. 47, No. 4). New York: BILL Communications, Inc.

World Tourism Organization. (1995). *Yearbook of Tourism Statistics–Volume 1* (47th ed.). Madrid, Spain: Author.

World Tourism Organization. (1997). *Yearbook of Tourism Statistics* (49th ed., Vol. 1). Madrid, Spain: Author.

World Tourism Organization. (1999). *Yearbook of Tourism Statistics* (51st ed., Vol. 1). Madrid, Spain: Author.

Convention Mythology

Heywood T. Sanders, PhD

SUMMARY. American cities are in the midst of a vast boom in convention center development. Communities from Hartford to San Francisco are building new or expanded centers with the goal of competing for conventions, tradeshows, and overnight visitors. That boom has been sustained by descriptions of a consistently growing demand for space, with increasing numbers of convention events and attendance, and the image of millions of dollars of local economic impact. The realities of the industry are often rather different. This article reviews the most widely employed measures of industry growth, as well as the impact of larger changes in 2001 and since. It examines the performance of major centers that have added new exhibit space in recent years and the evidence supporting forecasts of large scale economic impact and results. It concludes with an analysis of the current relationship between industry supply and demand, and the future of convention center investment. *[Article copies available for a fee from The Haworth Document Delivery Service: 1-800- HAWORTH. E-mail address: <docdelivery@haworthpress.com> Website: <http:// www.HaworthPress.com> © 2004 by The Haworth Press, Inc. All rights reserved.]*

KEYWORDS. Convention centers, trends, economic impact, convention industry, consultants, meeting planners, headquarters hotels

---

Heywood T. Sanders is Professor, Department of Public Administration, University of Texas at San Antonio, 501 West Durango, San Antonio, TX 78207.

[Haworth co-indexing entry note]: "Convention Mythology." Sanders, Heywood T. Co-published simultaneously in *Journal of Convention & Event Tourism* (The Haworth Hospitality Press, an imprint of The Haworth Press, Inc.) Vol. 6, No. 1/2, 2004, pp. 99-143; and: *Current Issues in Convention and Exhibition Facility Development* (ed: Robert R. Nelson) The Haworth Hospitality Press, an imprint of The Haworth Press, Inc., 2004, pp. 99-143. Single or multiple copies of this article are available for a fee from The Haworth Document Delivery Service [1-800-HAWORTH, 9:00 a.m. - 5:00 p.m. (EST). E-mail address: docdelivery@haworthpress.com].

http://www.haworthpress.com/web/JCET
Digital Object Identifier: 10.1300/J452v06n01_07

American cities are in the midst of a remarkable boom in convention center development. In 1992, major U.S. exhibit halls covered about 43.4 million square feet of exhibit space. By 2002, that total had reached 57.6 million–an increase of more than 14 million square feet or 33%. And the boom is continuing. One source has estimated that another 12 million square feet will be added to the North American exhibit hall inventory over the next few years, fueled by a substantial increase in convention center construction (*Tradeshow Week*, 2002a). New exhibit halls are underway in Boston, Washington, Pittsburgh, Richmond, New Orleans, Chicago, San Francisco, Dallas, Houston, and Portland. The total annual government spending on convention centers grew from $1.16 billion in 1993 to an estimated $2.48 billion in 2001 and $2.43 million for 2002 (U.S. Bureau of the Census, 2002).

For city after city, new or expanded convention center space appears to be the answer to a host of local problems and concerns. Center boosters argue that these facilities, by luring long staying, big spending visitors to a community, pay their cost back multiple times in economic impact and growth. Others see the promise of filled hotel rooms and the prospect of new private investment in hotels, restaurants, and visitor services. Beyond the issue of community-wide economic development, centers also hold out the promise of downtown renewal and revitalization as visitor activity and spending brings new life into urban cores. In the words of urban planner Alexander Garvin, "Cities invest in convention centers because they think they are municipal moneymaking machines" (Garvin, 2002, p. 102).

For all the public dollars committed to convention center development, their actual impact and import have not been seriously researched and studied. The development boom has rather been sustained by a number of myths, regularly perpetuated in consultants' feasibility and market studies and repeated from city to city by public officials and business leaders. This article seeks to review a number of those central myths and investigate the empirical evidence that supports or contradicts them. It concludes with a broader assessment of the convention industry and its future.

MYTH #1: THE PERPETUALLY GROWING INDUSTRY

For years, the convention and tradeshow industry has been described as "growing." A September 2002 publication of the industry's research and promotional arm, the Center for Exhibition Industry Research, argued that:

For the last 35 years continued growth of the exhibition industry has been a certainty. The question was never "Are we growing?" but rather

"How much did we grow?" Even during the last four recessions the industry boasted growth in the traditional industry metrics. . . . Historically, the addition of new facilities has triggered additional industry growth and it is reasonable to believe that will continue to be the case in the first decade of the 21st Century. (Center for Exhibition Industry Research, 2002, p. 4)

The argument for growth–in terms of events, exhibit space, and attendance–has also been common to consultants' feasibility studies. An analysis of the prospects for an expanded San Diego Convention Center completed by Price Waterhouse in September 1991 noted that "during the 1980s, the convention and tradeshow industry experienced increases in number of events, attendance, and required exhibit space" (Price Waterhouse, 1991, p. 3). It then estimated that the industry could anticipate a 7% increase in occupied exhibit space, and that "facilities in premier destinations have historically been able to add space and absorb it quickly (taking business from less popular destinations)" (Price Waterhouse, 1991, p. 8).

Baltimore, Maryland, got similar news from its consultant study in 1993, which concluded that "the annual growth rate in net square feet of exhibit space used averaged 7.3% between 1980 and 1991. . . . This indicates strong demand for larger spaces, although capacities of existing facilities act as a constraint to growth in square footage used" (Economics Research Associates, 1993, p. 11).

Optimism about industry growth has continued to the present, despite the economic travails of 2001 and the events of September 11, 2001. A February 2002 analysis for the city of Cincinnati argued that "overall, association convention and tradeshow industry trends continue to reflect general stability and new annual growth in terms of expenditures, attendance, and number of events. . . Within 12 to 24 months, growth in event and attendance activity is expected to resume . . . [and] steady event/attendance growth should continue" (Conventions, Sports and Leisure, 2002, n.p.).

The image of persistent growth is a powerful one, crucial to the promotion of ever larger convention centers. First, it implies that a growing level of demand makes it possible to fill up ever more space in new or expanded centers; that is, there is effectively little or no direct competition between centers for events or attendees. Or, as in the case of San Diego, it is argued that a "premier" destination can take convention business from less popular locales. One corollary of this part of the growth argument is that centers "lose business" because they are too small.

A second dimension of the growth argument is a new or expanded center can expect a growing business each year as new and larger events, with ever-greater attendance, come to the convention center. Based on this assumption a number of feasibility and market studies project steadily increasing activity and attendance for centers. For example, a 1988 study of a new convention center for Philadelphia argued that a survey of association executives indicated "that attendance will grow at a compound annual rate of approximately 4%," and thus projected that the center's 48 annual conventions and tradeshows would grow in attendance from 263,000 in 1994 to 346,000 by 2001 (Pannell Kerr Forster, 1988, p. VI-10).

Finally, market studies have regularly assumed that growth in the size of tradeshows and convention space usage obliges events to move to larger centers, outgrowing those centers that don't expand. A 1993 feasibility study for a new Washington Convention Center by Deloitte and Touche argued that continuing growth in event space requirements meant that "markets not increasing their supply of exhibit space to meet the increased size demands of expositions could fail to attract the lucrative business of the larger events," estimating that the average tradeshow would grow in size and attendance more than 4% each year from 1991 to 2001 (Deloitte and Touche, 1993, p. 39). The Deloitte analysis concluded that "given this growth, the Washington Convention Center will have difficulty attracting even the average-sized show in the future" (Deloitte and Touche, 1993, p. 33).

The growth argument has commonly been sustained by data from three principal sources. *Meetings and Conventions* magazine conducts a biennial survey of meeting planners, which provides broad information on the number of events, annual attendance, and expenditures. *Tradeshow Week* conducts both an annual survey of planned convention and tradeshow events, and a detailed assessment of the 200 largest events each year. Each of these sources provides a distinct, if not necessarily comparable, index to the size and change in the industry.

The "Meetings Market Survey" has long held a central place in consultant studies. Focusing on the part of that survey most relevant to convention centers, the count and size of association conventions, a November 1995 study by Stein and Company of center expansion for Austin, Texas, noted that "since 1991, conventions have experienced the most dramatic growth with a 16% increase in the number of events, a 24% increase in attendance, and a 41% increase in direct spending" (Stein and Company, 1995, Section 4, p. 15). The same language would appear the following year in a Stein and Company feasibility study for Milwaukee, Wisconsin (Stein and Company, 1996). And exactly the same language appears in a March 1997 study by C. H. Johnson (now with his own firm) of a new Boston convention center. And C. H. Johnson Consulting employed the same data, albeit not the percentage increase discussion, in a market analysis for a new center in Buffalo, New York, completed in December 1997.

Other consultants, including the former Coopers & Lybrand, have also employed the "Meetings Market Survey" results. Thus, a September 1996 analysis of public assembly facilities for the city of Fort Worth, Texas, presented tabular data on meetings and attendance, noting that "from 1993 to 1995, attendance was up 22% for conventions" and concluding that "the overall industry trends serve to highlight the stability and overall steady growth patterns of the convention and meeting industry" (Coopers & Lybrand, 1996, p. B-2, p. B-4). A similar study by Coopers the following year for Washington, D.C., concluded that "the overall long-term trend of the convention and trade show industry is one of sustained growth marked by occasional periods of lower growth in response to downswings in the nation's economy" (Coopers & Lybrand, 1997a, p. 9).

Convention attendance indexed by the survey did indeed jump 24% from 1991 to 1993, recovering from the trough of the Gulf War economic downturn. And from 1993 to 1995, there was yet another serious increase, raising the convention attendance figure to 13 million. Yet the 1995, attendance total was actually less than in 1985 and 1989. And since 1995 there has been no evidence of a consistent growth trend in either number of conventions or total attendance, as shown in Figures 1 and 2. Indeed, the count of total events for 2001 is just equal to 1993's total and less than in the last half of the 1980s.

Despite the fact that the "Meetings Market Survey" data do not justify a conclusion of regular or predictable growth, they continue to be employed in supporting new convention centers and related hotel projects. A September 2002 study by PKF of a potential 1,500 room convention headquarters hotel for San Antonio, Texas, used the data for just 1997, 1999, and 2001 to conclude that "While the rate of growth has slowed, the increase of meeting activity over the two-year period 1999 through 2001 is a positive sign for the meetings industry" (PKF, 2002a, Sec. III, p. 6).

A second major source of industry data is the annual the *Tradeshow Week Data Book*. The *Data Book*, issued prior to the year it is dated, contains an elaborate index to convention and tradeshow events, together with information on attendance, space use, and number of exhibitors. The Center for Exhibition Industry Research has long employed the annual figures from the *Data Book* to make the argument of persistent growth. For example, the Center's 1996 review of the size of exhibition industry predicted growth in the number of events to 4,781 by 2000 (or about 8.7%), with a total attendance of 140 million–a gain of 39% from the 101 million attendees estimated for 1996. A subsequent 1998 report forecast 4,970 events and 157 million attendees by 2002 (Center for Exhibition Industry Research, 1998).

FIGURE 1. Meetings Market Conventions by Year

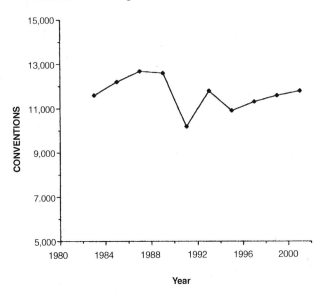

Source: *Meetings & Conventions, Meetings Market Report*, selected years

But the projections of the Center failed to materialize. The *Data Book* counted 4,637 events in 2000, a total that fell to just 4,342 for 2002. Attendance, projected to reach 140 million for 2000, was estimated at 126 million for that year, dropping to 75 million in 2001 and just 56 million in 2002.

The total event counts from the Center for Exhibition Industry Research and the *Data Book* have some basis in an annual survey of exhibition organizers. They provide one estimate of the scale and direction of the industry. But as Figure 3 indicates, the recent totals for events show no real increase since the mid-1990s. The 2002 figure is almost exactly the same as in 1994 and 1995.

The *Data Book*'s figures for attendance are merely estimates from some event organizers produced up to a year prior to an event. *Tradeshow Week* does not even get estimates for all 4,000 plus events. It simply takes the average estimates–for future attendance and space use–of those who supply them, and then multiplies the averages by the event total. Essentially these constitute a multiplied set of guesses, rather than any reliable index of industry performance or activity.

The third major source of convention industry performance data is *Tradeshow Week*'s annual compilation of the top 200 events, the *Tradeshow Week 200*. The *Tradeshow Week 200* is a post-hoc summary, and thus avoids the "guess" problem of the larger *Data Book*, although it, by definition, focuses on

FIGURE 2. Meetings Market Convention Attendance by Year

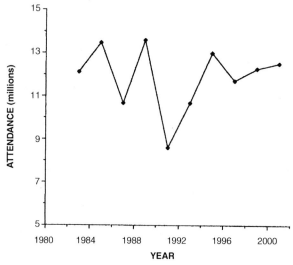

Source: *Meetings & Conventions, Meetings Market Report*, selected years

FIGURE 3. Convention and Tradeshow Events by Year

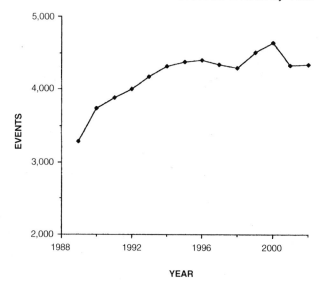

Source: *Tradeshow Week, Tradeshow Week Data Book*, selected years

the largest events. If an event fails to grow sufficiently in terms of exhibit space, it will simply fall out of the *Tradeshow Week 200*. In 1993, Price Waterhouse assessed the tradeshow market for a new Boston center as follows:

> Growth for the country's largest 200 trade shows, all of which require more than 225,000 gross square feet of exhibition space, has been similar to growth for the entire U.S. trade show industry. . . . Based on these industry trends and notwithstanding the effects of the current economic recession, there is currently no persuasive evidence that exhibition space demand for either trade shows or conventions will abate in the near future. (Price Waterhouse, 1993, p. 25)

A subsequent Price Waterhouse analysis of an expanded Georgia World Congress Center in 1996 noted that "annual attendance growth at the *Tradeshow Week 200* over the past 10 years has averaged approximately 4.0%, while net square feet of exhibit space occupied has grown at a slightly higher pace of approximately 5.0%, on average" (Price Waterhouse, 1996b, p. 56). Using the performance of *Tradeshow Week's* 200, KPMG concluded that a new Arizona convention center would be able to take advantage of "strong tradeshow industry growth for future years due to the healthy U.S. economy and the surging stock market" (KPMG, 1998, p. 13). It then argued that:

> Over the past two decades, exhibit space requirements and number of attendees to tradeshows have been increasing, and this trend is expected to continue. As tradeshows grow in size, meeting planners may choose larger venues for their events. The growing number of large tradeshows indicates a future need for larger exhibit facilities. (KPMG, 1998, p. 22)

The promise of growth for the largest events thus involves both concurrent annual increases in attendance and space use and the notion that convention centers which seek to compete for business must "keep up" by adding ever more space. Figures 4 and 5 indicate the total net square feet of exhibit space used by year, as well as the annual attendance total, for *Tradeshow Week's* 200 events. Space clearly has steadily increased during the 1990s through the year 2000, followed by a clear drop in 2001. Attendance, in contrast, grew to a peak of over 5 million in 1996, followed by a modest decline and stable levels through 2000. As with space, attendance fell in 2001, by about 10%.

Tradeshow Week (2002b) consistently reported growth in exhibit space and attendance from 1992 through 2000. But behind the image of growth is a rather more complex tale. While total exhibit space used grew from almost 57 million in 1995 to 69.75 million in 2002–about 23%–the median-sized *Tradeshow Week 200* event grew from 221,750 square feet to 267,677–about

FIGURE 4. "200" Event Space Use by Year

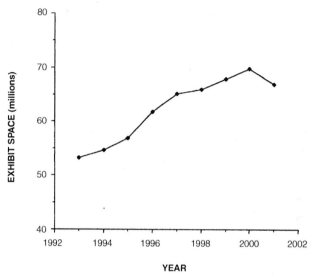

Source: *Tradeshow Week, Tradeshow Week 200*, selected years

FIGURE 5. "200" Event Attendance by Year

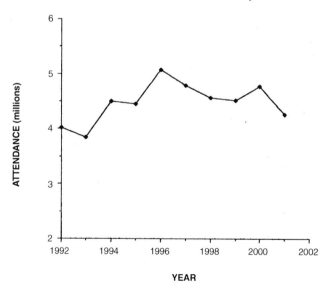

Source: *Tradeshow Week, Tradeshow Week 200*, selected years

21%. Most of that growth for the median-sized event occurred between 1995 and 1997. From 1997 to 2000, as Figure 6 indicates, there was no real growth at the middle of the 200 largest events. Similarly, the smallest event to make it into the *Tradeshow Week 200* for 1995 used 125,000 square feet of exhibit space. That reached 143,000 for 1997. But for 2000, the smallest *Tradeshow Week 200* event was just 144,000 square feet, falling back to 143,000 in 2001.

While there was growth in the aggregate for the *Tradeshow Week*'s 200, those events that are more typical of the larger convention and tradeshow industry, at the middle and bottom of *Tradeshow Week*'s 200, demonstrated no real growth in exhibit space use after 1997. An examination of 149 of the *Tradeshow Week 200* events which consistently appeared in the listings for 1996, 1998, and 2000 makes clear why an aggregate analysis of all 200 of the top convention and trade events can be misleading. Although the average (mean) event size for 1996 among these consistent events was 319,913 square feet, the median was just 250,000. The largest cluster of events fell under 200,000 square feet–a group including 53 of the 149. Another 19 events fell in the range of 200,000 to 250,000 square feet, with 22 between 250,000 and 300,000 square feet. Thus, even among the 200 largest conventions and tradeshows–the industry's leaders–the overall size distribution is a pyramid, with a large number of events at the smallest size levels and just a handful of

FIGURE 6. Median and Smallest "200" Event Space Use by Year

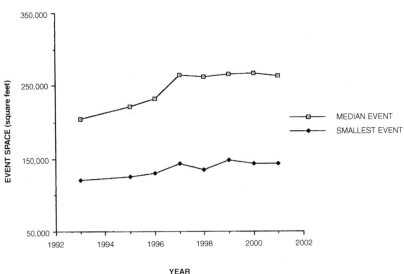

Source: *Tradeshow Week, Tradeshow Week 200,* selected years

very large events. Indeed, just 20 of the consistent events exceeded 500,000 square feet of exhibit space in 1996.

Far from a booming and regularly growing industry, the overall convention and tradeshow market has shown no consistent growth in the total count of events in recent years, based on either the "Meetings Market Survey" or *Data Book* data. Space use, one of the central foundation stones of the convention center boom, appears to have been effectively flat since about 1997. And convention attendance, based on either the *Tradeshow Week 200* totals or the "Meetings Market Survey" data, appears to have been at best stable in recent years. It is possible to employ a limited selection of years to provide some evidence of growth or to focus on a subset of events. But the broad evidence from the middle of the 1990s suggests that the question "Are we growing?" is best answered with a "No."

MYTH #2: THE CURRENT DECLINE AND THE COMING TURNAROUND

The year 2001 clearly represents a watershed in the recent history of the convention and tradeshow industry. Between the impact of recession and corporate restructuring in the first half of the year, and the events of September 11, any industry linked to travel and meetings saw significant change. The *Tradeshow Week 200* covering all of 2001 reported the "steepest declines in the directory's history," with a 1.3% decrease in adjusted exhibit space use and a 4.5% decline in adjusted attendance. The last quarter of the year, reflecting the September 11 terrorist events, was reported to show an 8.6% drop in net square footage and a 20.4% fall in attendance.

The situation for the first half of 2002 appears somewhat less dire, although *Tradeshow Week*'s quarterly report for the second quarter of 2002 indicated a 6.2% decline in space use and a 6.0% drop in attendance from a year earlier.

Still, many in the industry remain quite optimistic about the future and a return to the assumed pattern of consistent growth. The Center for Exhibition Industry Research's September 2002 analysis concludes that "the future of the exhibition industry is bright" (Center for Exhibition Industry Research, 2002, p. 3). *Tradeshow Week*'s (Dodds, 2002) report on the first quarter of 2002 was headlined "Shows continue to shrink, but recovery may be at hand." And a number of consultant studies completed in 2002 continue to forecast growth. For example, PKF's September 2002 headquarters hotel analysis for San Antonio concludes that meeting expenditures and attendance "are returning to previous levels achieved in the early to mid-1990s" (PKF, 2002a, Sec. III, p. 6).

A review of the broader evidence on the industry in 2001 and 2002 paints a somewhat different picture. The change in 2001, even in the first half of that year, appears larger than the figures from *Tradeshow Week* indicate.

Tradeshow Week bases its analysis of percentage change for the *Tradeshow Week 200* on the difference between an adjusted figure for the prior year and the performance of the year under review, only for those events which are comparable over the two years. But the prior year figures are almost invariably lower than reported a year earlier. For example, the April 2001 report on events in 2000 showed a total space used of 69.75 million. A year later, the reported 2000 space use had dropped to 67.64 million square feet–a change of more than 2 million square feet. By using a revised figure for the prior year as the base, the change percentages tend to be inflated.

A comparison of total exhibit space use from 2000–reported at 69.75 million square feet–to a 2001 total of 66.985 million square feet means that exhibit space used actually dropped by 3.97%. A parallel comparison of annual attendance totals shows a decline from 4.77 million attendees in 2000 to just 4.266 million in 2001, or 10.62%. These losses are far greater than the published figures (1.3% and 4.5%, respectively), and suggest that 2001 represents a far more dramatic change in the industry overall.

A parallel analysis, based on a stable set of 125 events from 1996 through 2001, also indicates a real sea change. For the 98 events that occurred prior to September 11, 2001, overall exhibit space was almost unchanged from the previous year, at a slight increase of 0.51%. Attendance showed a slight drop of 0.21%. But for the 27 events that took place after September 11, overall exhibit space use dropped by 8.8%. Attendance showed a sharp drop of 25.4% from the prior year. The import of these figures is that even before September 11, the industry's major events were flat in terms of space use and attendance. As for most of the travel and hospitality industry, the impact of September 11 was a dramatic shift in individual travel behavior and tradeshow performance.

The independent impacts of both the economy and the events of September 11 can also be seen in the attendance data from some of the country's major convention centers. Any analysis that relies upon selected individual cases is subject to questions of reliability and selectivity (Are they reasonable representatives?). The convention centers discussed here have long been seen as successful and regularly growing in terms of activity and market share. Their performance during 2001 and 2002 should provide a reasonable–indeed, conservative–picture of recent center performance.

Take the case of Atlanta's Georgia World Congress Center, one of the largest and most successful centers in the nation, described by consultant David Petersen as "the premier facility of its kind in the southeastern United States" (Petersen, 2001, p. 213). The World Congress Center has long had an impressive performance record in terms of events and attendance. And since it maintains attendance records on a fiscal year basis, it provides a measure of the performance of a successful center for the last half of calendar year 2000 and the first half of 2001, prior to the September 11 events.

After a major expansion was completed in 1993, the center hosted almost 750,000 convention and tradeshow attendees in fiscal 1994 and 879,000 the following year. Attendance was affected by the Olympic games in 1996, but rose to almost 838,000 in fiscal 1997. As Table 1 indicates, the World Congress Center has been unable to match either the 1995 or the 1997 attendance totals in the years since. The World Congress Center's convention and tradeshow attendance in fiscal 2000 was about 716,000 and just under 725,000 the next year. Thus, prior to September 11, the attendance trend at the World Congress Center was flat.

For fiscal year 2002, obviously affected by September 11 and its aftermath, convention attendance came to just 569,887–a drop of 21.4% for the year. That constitutes a rather larger attendance loss than the national figures based on the *Tradeshow Week 200* events suggest.

A similar case is evident on the west coast with another successful major convention venue, San Francisco's Moscone Convention Center. The recent pattern of convention and tradeshow events and attendance at Moscone, on a fiscal year basis, is shown in Table 2. For 1996/1997, Moscone housed 51 events with total attendance just over 705,000. Totals reached 56 events and

TABLE 1. Georgia World Congress Center Annual Attendance

Fiscal Year	Convention and Tradeshow Attendance	
1991	637,000	
1992		
1993	677,322	Expansion Opened
1994	749,656	
1995	879,036	
1996	562,000	Attendance Reduced by Olympics
1997	837,752	
1998	672,425	
1999	723,284	
2000	715,914	
2001	724,677	
2002	569,887	

Source: Georgia World Congress Center Authority.

TABLE 2. Moscone Convention Center Events and Attendance

Year	Events	Attendance
1991/2	47	442,525
1992/3	58	599,044
1993/4	52	666,976
1994/5	62	649,967
1995/6	61	628,564
1996/7	51	705,358
1997/8	56	728,771
1998/9	61	790,548
1999/2000	51	573,417
2000/1	52	737,694
2001/2	45	626,108

Source: Moscone Center annual reports.

almost 729,000 attendees the following year. By 1998/1999, the center hit 61 events and over 790,000 attendees. But after a sharp drop in fiscal 2000 to about 573,000, the totals for 2000/2001 (before September 11) were just 52 events and attendance of 737,694.

The attendance and event figures for the Moscone center do not suggest a steadily growing industry. They do support the conclusion that even before the terrorist attacks of September 11, 2001, the industry was effectively flat in terms of attendance since the middle of the 1990s.

The impact of September 11 and its aftermath are clearly visible in Moscone Center's convention and tradeshow performance for fiscal year 2002. The event total dropped to 45, the lowest in a decade. Attendance fell to 626,108, a drop of just over 15% from the previous year and the lowest since fiscal 1993.

Orlando, Florida, offers yet another case of the actual performance of a highly successful, high demand center (see Table 3). The Orlando/Orange County Convention Center has succeeded in expanding its overall size and exhibit space, eventually reaching over 1 million square feet of exhibit area in 1998. That year, it hosted 115 convention and tradeshow events and more than 837,000 attendees. By 1999, it reached totals of 120 events and almost 892,000 attendees, and for 2000 the event count stood at 116 with attendance of 921,247.

For calendar year 2001, the Orlando center's total event count fell to 105, with 702,404 attendees. That amounted to a 9.5% drop in events for the year and a decrease in convention attendance of 23.76%. Orlando's experience very much parallels that of the Georgia World Congress Center, with a dramatic attendance decline for the full year in excess of 20%. A review of figures

TABLE 3. Orlando/Orange County Convention Center Events and Attendance

Year	Events	Attendance
1983	12	55,440
1984	16	163,707
1985	23	155,213
1986	30	201,560
1987	24	145,368
1988	34	218,827
1989	60	342,770
1990	66	376,973
1991	58	314,802
1992	66	425,950
1993	73	396,218
1994	81	499,572
1995	82	485,722
1996	114	848,911
1997	121	758,967
1998	115	837,611
1999	120	891,873
2000	116	921,247
2001	105	702,404

Source: Orlando/Orange County Convention and Visitors Bureau.

for the first 6 months of the year, covering all events at the Orlando/Orange County Center, where some 85% of attendance is generated by conventions and tradeshows, also provides a clearer sense of the independent impact of the 2001 recession and forces prior to September 11.

From January through June 1998, the Orlando center attracted attendance of just over 530,000. By 2001, the first 6 months' total came to 559,275. But for the first half of 2001, attendance came to just 490,425–a drop of more than 12.3% from a year earlier. Even before September, the recently expanded Orlando center witnessed a significant attendance decline.

For 2002, the January through June attendance total came to 501,704. That figure represents a 2.3% increase from the previous year and suggests something of a return to normality. But roughly 502,000 attendees in the first half is less than in any year since 1998.

Clearly, based on both national figures and the performance of selected individual centers, the industry decline in 2001 reflected both a sharp impact of economic forces and the September 11 events, with each contributing to dramatic attendance declines. The question for the future is the prospect of turnaround in an environment where industry consultants confidently predict a return to the presumed pattern of steady growth. In part, that question can be answered through an assessment of the performance of major events thus far in 2002.

Tradeshow Week's analysis of industry performance for the first quarter of 2002 noted declines in every standard performance measure from the previous year, albeit the declines show "signs of slowing when compared with the rate at which shows shrank from the third to fourth quarters of 2001 . . . [indicating] an improvement in the tradeshow industry" (Dodds, 2002, p. 1, p. 7). The change figures from the previous year included a 5.5% decrease in net square footage and a drop in attendance of 8.1%.

Tradeshow Week's quarterly analysis examines events with at least 30,000 square feet of paid exhibit space. But the number of events, and the events included, vary from year to year. And the year-to-year comparison is based on event organizers' reports of previous year figures, which often differ from those reported the previous year. The result is often to blur the actual level of change in industry.

In order to provide a more stable basis of comparison, I extracted those events reporting first quarter performance for 2002 that were in turn included in the *Tradeshow Week 200* for 2001. This group of 45 tradeshows provides a more stable and consistent set of major events, where the current quarter report can be compared to the actual report for the previous year, rather than a revised figure or no report at all. The result of that analysis, and a comparison with the published figures, is shown in Table 4. The declines in both exhibit space and attendance for major events are clearly far more substantial than *Tradeshow Week*'s published figures.

TABLE 4. Convention and Tradeshow Industry Performance First Quarter 2002 Compared to First Quarter 2001

	Tradeshow Week Report	"200" Event Data (N = 45)
Change in:		
Exhibit Space	−5.5%	−8.89%
Attendance	−8.1%	−14.84%

Source: *Tradeshow Week*, May 6, 2002.

A parallel analysis of the second and third quarters of 2002, again based on *Tradeshow Week*'s 200 events, is shown in Table 5. Exhibit space use in the second quarter shows a drop of 8.6% from the previous year, while attendance is down by 9.14%, in both cases exceeding the reported quarterly changes. The third quarter of 2002 shows a rather more modest decrease, with space use down 4.4% and attendance down 4.96%. The third quarter figures, however, reflect the impact of events held after September 11, 2001. These events would, of course, show a substantial drop from 2000, and thus constitute an unusually low base figure for an examination of change. Eliminating the post-September 11 events and including those for July, August, and early September, exhibit space use shows a change of −5.57%, with attendance at −7.76%.

The quarterly change figures for 2002, based on major industry events, show a pattern of continuing declines in attendance and exhibit space from the previous year, declines that are larger than published analyses. Given the magnitude and consistency of these declines, the recovery of the industry is likely to be more limited and delayed than commonly projected.

The sharp change in convention industry performance in 2001 was obviously a dual result of forces outside the industry. The impact of those forces, on both leading events and the performance of some major centers, was dramatic. But the lingering effects of economic change and altered travel habits may well persist for an extended period. At the very least, it is clear that the downturn was even more substantial than some analyses have concluded, and thus may last rather longer. And it remains an open question as to whether a "turnaround" means a return to regular growth or to the pattern of effectively flat industry performance during the 1997 to 2000 period.

TABLE 5. Convention and Tradeshow Industry Performance Second and Third Quarter 2002 Compared to 2001

"200" Events

	Second Quarter	Third Quarter	Third Quarter Before 9/11
	(N = 24)	(N = 26)	(N = 21)
Change in Exhibit Space	−8.58%	−4.39%	−5.57%
Change in Attendance	−9.14%	−4.96%	−7.76%

Source: *Tradeshow Week*, September 9, 2002 and November 11, 2002.

MYTH #3: THE RELIABLE CONSULTANT FORECAST

From Anaheim to Austin, Atlanta to Albany, and Washington, D.C., to Seattle, Washington, the public discussion about convention center investment is shaped around feasibility and market studies done by a small set of industry consultants. In each of these cities, and dozens of others, the consultant feasibility study provided a review of the overall convention and tradeshow market, an assessment of the competitive position of the individual city under study, and some estimates of likely business and, in many cases, economic impact.

In places like Austin and Fort Worth, Cincinnati and Nashville, political, business and civic leaders employ the findings of those studies to promote convention-oriented investment, arguing that a new center or more space will "attract more conferences to our city that will bring more visitors who will use our hotels, eat in our restaurants, shop in our stores, and support our arts" (San Jose, California, mayor, Ron Gonzales, as cited in Roberts, 2002).

The promise of more visitors and more dollars is a strikingly attractive one, carrying the prospect of local economic growth, new private investment in things like hotels and restaurants, and the revitalization of the area surrounding the convention center. And although the persistent findings of such studies–in cities as different as Buffalo and Minneapolis–that more and newer convention center space will invariably generate more events, more attendees, and more spending might be open to question, there are few individuals in a position to critically assess and analyze the methodology and conclusions of the studies.

The two central issues in assessing the reliability and substance of these market and feasibility studies are how effectively they capture the competitive situation of a city and how closely their forecasts–of event activity, visitors, and overnight hotel stays–come to being realized. Each individual consultant brings his or her own methodology and approach to the assessment of a city's and a center's competitive position and likely success. For some, prior success in attracting conventions and tradeshows is seen as an effective predictor of future success. Thus a recent analysis by PriceWaterhouseCoopers of a new convention and exhibition center under construction in Boston noted that evidenced by:

> Boston's past success as a convention destination, the high occupancy of the Hynes Convention Center, strength of the local hotel market, variety of destination amenities, and other characteristics illustrated in this section, Boston has been and is expected to continue to be a successful convention and visitor destination. (PriceWaterhouseCoopers, 2002, Sec. II, p. 13)

The PriceWaterhouseCoopers study also noted that Boston had a favorable position in terms of total hotel function space, ranked eighth among 16 comparable destination cities in terms of metropolitan area hotel room supply, and ranked seventh in the same group in terms of number of direct airline flights. The study then concluded that "Boston has the destination characteristics necessary to compete for additional conventions and trade shows not previously possible" (PriceWaterhouseCoopers, 2002, Sec. III, p. 12).

But cities that have not been notably successful in luring conventions and tradeshows also can be judged to have sufficient promise to build new convention centers. PriceWaterhouseCoopers argued in 2001 that "there is sufficient market demand for the development of a new Cleveland convention center with a building program offering up to 400,000 square feet of exhibit space" (PriceWaterhouseCoopers, 2001, p. i). That assessment came despite the conclusion that "Cleveland's convention and trade show occupancy compares poorly to competitive destinations" (PriceWaterhouseCoopers, 2001, p. i). The positive assessment came in part because the consultant compared Cleveland to a very different set of destination cities than Boston. Where Boston stood out for its supply of some 6,287 hotel rooms within one mile of the existing Hynes Center, Cleveland's proximate hotel room supply came to just 2,421–far less than the 4,082 in St. Louis, the 4,472 in Baltimore, or the 3,059 in Cincinnati–and apparently not a deterrent to center development.

Indeed, Cincinnati, which has long underperformed as a convention destination, is now armed with a set of feasibility studies justifying the expansion of its convention center despite its previous performance. A 1999 analysis by PriceWaterhouse Coopers noted that "Cincinnati has lost major groups . . . and smaller groups (such as SMERF groups) have replaced them" (PriceWaterhouseCoopers, 1999, p. 22). But an assessment of its "destination resources," including proximate retail and hotels, hotel taxes, and costs, appeared to rank the city well among its competitors. On 10 items, Cincinnati ranked 5.2 (1 equals highest) among 15 competitors. Cleveland, examined by the same firm not long after the Cincinnati study, came in at 6.9. And Nashville, which is armed with yet another feasibility study from a different consultant, came in at a ranking of 9.9.

A more recent study of Cincinnati's prospects by the Conventions, Sports and Leisure firm (CSL) in 2002 found that the city has "the long-term potential to support up to 350,000 square feet of exhibit space," but that a smaller expansion to a 200,000 square foot exhibit hall with extensive improvements "could add 15 percentage points to market capture" (Conventions, Sports and Leisure, 2002, n.p.). One of the methods CSL employed in assessing Cincinnati's potential was a survey of event planners, asking whether they would use an expanded convention center for their future events. Summing the "positive response percentage" of those who answered definitely use, likely use, or possibly use yielded a figure for Cincinnati of 39%.

The CSL analysis of Cincinnati's potential business then noted that the 39% figure "is one of the lowest recorded by CSL during industry surveys for similar studies," comparing it to Kansas City (60%), Boston (56%), and Nashville (62%). Yet even with that dismal rating by the potential consumers of an expanded center, CSL urged the city to move ahead, arguing that "a combination of significant physical and technological improvements to the center, strategic expansion of key elements of the center, and increasing marketing highlighting such improvements and other city amenities will be required in the short-term" (Conventions, Sports and Leisure, 2002, n.p.).

Just as in the case of PriceWaterhouseCoopers' studies, a strong positive response by meeting planners may be a boost to a city's competitive prospects. When CSL (1999a) surveyed event planners about the likelihood of using space in Nashville, the "positive response percentage of 62%" appeared to justify up to 400,000 square feet of exhibit space. And the response of planners ranked Nashville in the middle of 14 comparable cities in terms of delegate drawing power. But the fact that the same survey placed Cincinnati tied with Tampa for next to last (Houston) was presumably not relevant to Cincinnati's future prospects or CSL's 2002 Cincinnati study.

Indeed, the CSL method of surveying meeting planners, using the same approach a firm principal employed during some years with Coopers & Lybrand, can be stretched to justify the conclusion that more convention center space will work for any city. For Nashville, positive response percentages for events of different sizes ranged from 50% to 67%. Yet a similar analysis by Coopers & Lybrand of Minneapolis in 1994 yielded positive response percentages ranging from 24% to 59% across varying event sizes, significantly less. The conclusion of Coopers: "Compared to surveys conducted in similar markets throughout the country, these percentages indicate a higher than average positive response towards holding an event in Minneapolis," supporting an estimate that the city could attract 32% of national/regional events (Coopers & Lybrand, 1994, p. 32). Based in part on those survey results, the Coopers study called for an expansion of the Minneapolis Convention Center up to 500,000 square feet of exhibit space, roughly doubling its size.

The relatively weak response of meeting planners to Minneapolis was thus not irremediable. The Coopers study went on to conclude that while "45% to 55% [of the planners' negative responses] reflected conditions that would be difficult to overcome, . . . the remaining concerns, including weather, lack of members, travel distance, and others, could represent perceptions of the city which may be overcome by specific marketing efforts" (Coopers & Lybrand, 1994, p. 37).

The optimism of this consultant had been equally evident a year earlier, in a study for the Commonwealth of Massachusetts of a convention center in Boston. There, the positive response percentages had ranged from 21% for small events up to 56% for large events, averaging about 33%. These numbers appeared even worse than those for Minneapolis, and Coopers & Lybrand agreed, mentioning that "these positive response percentages are not particularly high compared to similar markets" (Coopers & Lybrand, 1993, p. 25). Yet they still did not represent a serious problem:

> Approximately 40% to 50% of the negative responses could be attributable to region and weather factors. Many of the other factors, such as lack of event history, cost, union issues, familiarity, and other such items, could be mitigated to some degree through marketing efforts. (Coopers & Lybrand, 1993, p. 40)

Coopers & Lybrand also examined the expansion possibilities for New York City's Jacob Javits Convention Center (JKJCC), employing the same survey methodology in an April 1997 study. New York's positive response percentages varied from 33% to 62%, averaging out to 36%. That would place New York at about the same place as Cincinnati or Minneapolis, and perhaps a bit above Boston. But once again, Coopers concluded that "approximately 61% of the reasons given for not rotating to JKJCC could potentially be mitigated with facility management, marketing, and/or area development initiatives" (Coopers & Lybrand, 1997a, Section 5, p. 5). The penultimate conclusion of the Coopers & Lybrand New York City analysis:

> Given the past success realized by the JKJCC in the trade and public show market, there appears to be a significant opportunity for New York to solidify and enhance its standing as a major trade event destination and to expand its event potential into the large scale convention market. (Coopers & Lybrand, 1997a, Executive Summary, p. i)

Such optimism about the convention and tradeshow market and local competitiveness would appear to have been contagious. Just a few months later, in December 1997, Coopers & Lybrand endorsed a new convention center in Washington, D.C., armed with a positive response percentage averaging 68% and concluding that:

> Given the WCC's past success in the international, national, and regional convention and trade show market, there appears to be a significant opportunity for Washington, D.C., to solidify and enhance its standing as a major convention destination. (Coopers & Lybrand, 1997b, p. 1)

From PriceWaterhouse to Coopers & Lybrand, CSL, and a host of other consultants, cities with records of convention success are told that more space will generate more business. And cities with only limited success, like Cleveland and Cincinnati, are also promised that more will bring more. Cities with high positive response ratings like Nashville and Washington get support for convention center development. And cities with demonstrably low ratings receive substantially the same advice.

The persistent enthusiasm of consultants for a whole range of cities–including places as diverse as Raleigh, North Carolina; Omaha, Nebraska; St. Charles, Missouri; Austin, Texas; Overland Park, Kansas; as well as Washington, New York, and San Diego–raises a host of questions about the ability of each of these locales to compete and the depth of the analyses they have received. Yet these consultants maintain a consistent positive outlook about the virtues and impact of convention center development and the future of the meetings industry.

In May 2001, the Strategic Advisory Group recommended that Schaumburg, Illinois, build a new convention center with 100,000 square feet of exhibit space attached to a new 500 room headquarter hotel. Their study argued that "over the first 30 years of operation, the Phase I complex will generate over $8.6 billion in new spending in the community," support 4,500 jobs, and "add a great deal to the social fabric of Schaumburg" (Strategic Advisory Group, 2001a, p. 3). The Strategic Advisory Group went on to describe "The Big Picture":

> When considering building new centers, community leadership often looks for the direct increment to local jurisdictional taxes related to the convention center to support the debt service and operating costs of the project. If this were to be the ultimate measure, very few convention centers in the U.S. would get developed. . . . This begs the question: what can communities do to strengthen their tourism base? Convention centers are the choice of most cities even in light of the public investment required beyond those generated by the delegate spending. Why? A convention center will drive room nights. . . . The economic impact of convention centers is much broader than what is captured by the local taxing structures relative to delegate spending alone. A convention center is one piece of an overall economic development strategy. . . Many impacts cannot be quantified. Consider a business looking to locate in Schaumburg. The proposed complex would offer an impressive statement to prospective clients for both business and quality of life reasons. (Strategic Advisory Group, 2001a, p. 132)

That conclusion reflected the firm's assessment of the national market: Industry experts see continued strong demand growth and interviews with meeting planners support this claim. But many believe that demand for space could slow or flatten after ten years or so as the industry matures. . . . The future growth in square footage demand and attendance is expected to be in the 3.5% range over the next several years. . . . Overall, supply and demand should stay in equilibrium. Top destinations should have full buildings for the foreseeable future. . . . In summary, the industry is healthy and growing, and is expected to continue to grow for at least a decade. No real threats appear to be on the horizon. (Strategic Advisory Group, 2001a, p. 13)

A few months later, in a December 17, 2001, report, the Strategic Advisory Group advised Albany, New York, that it should build a convention center with 60,000 square feet of exhibit space as the first phase of a 125,000 square foot planned center. Their study argued that such a center would "generate approximately $3.2 billion in total spending in the local economy over its first 30 years of operations, support 1,740 new jobs, and serve as an important piece of future downtown development activity" (Strategic Advisory Group, 2001b, pp. 4-5).

The Albany market analysis concluded with "The Big Picture" quite similar to Schaumburg:

When considering building new centers, community leadership often looks for the direct increment to local jurisdictional taxes related to the convention center to support the debt service and operating costs of the project. If this were to be the ultimate measure, very few convention centers in the U.S. would get developed. . . . This begs the question: what can communities do to strengthen their tourism base? Convention centers are the choice of most cities even in light of the public investment required beyond those generated by the delegate spending. Why? A convention center drives room nights and visitation. . . . The economic impact of convention centers is much broader than what is captured by the local taxing structures relative to delegate spending alone. A convention center is one piece of an overall economic development strategy. . . . Many impacts cannot be quantified. Often quality of life is an important consideration with respect to a convention center. Consider a business looking to locate in Albany. The proposed center would offer an impressive statement to prospective clients for both business and quality of life reasons. (Strategic Advisory Group, 2001b, pp. 79-80)

The consulting firm's December 2001 evaluation of Albany's convention prospects was rooted in a detailed assessment of the national meetings industry, one that must have reflected the economic changes underway during 2001, as well as the impact of September 11, some three months prior to the date of the report, and its effect on travel and meetings:

Industry experts see continued strong demand growth, and interviews with meeting planners support this claim. But many believe that demand for space could slow or flatten after 10 years or so as the industry matures. . . . The future growth in square footage demand and attendance is expected to be in the 3.5% range over the next several years. . . . Overall, supply and demand should stay in equilibrium. Top destinations should have full buildings for the foreseeable future. . . . In summary, the industry is healthy and growing, and is expected to grow for at least a decade. No real threats appear to be on the horizon. (Strategic Advisory Group, 2001b, pp. 15-16)

MYTH #4: MORE SPACE MEANS MORE BUSINESS

The combination of political rhetoric and optimistic feasibility studies has long fueled efforts to build more convention center space. But the question remains: Does more exhibit space mean more business, greater attendance, and increasing economic impact? There has been almost no substantial research examining the performance of convention centers over time, as they build expansions and add new space. It is possible to review the performance of a small group of expanding centers and provide at least a partial, initial answer. Again, this discussion of specific centers is necessarily selective, although it focuses on centers that have long been industry leaders in terms of size and success. Thus David Petersen (2001, p. 204) noted that for Chicago's McCormick Place, "The size of trade shows and the number of companies exhibiting at them increased as fast as McCormick Place could expand to accommodate the demand."

Chicago

Few cities have been as consistent and aggressive in adding exhibition space as Chicago with its McCormick Place Convention Center. Long the nation's largest convention facility, McCormick Place was originally built in 1960, then rebuilt and expanded after a fire in 1967. It then added an entirely new North Hall, with an additional 510,000 square feet in 1986. With a $987 million bond program in 1992, the Metropolitan Pier and Exposition Authority constructed the new South Hall with another 840,000 square feet of exhibit space. McCormick Place South opened in December 1996. And today, development is underway on McCormick Place West, designed to add another 600,000 square feet of exhibit space to the complex at a cost of some $800 million.

Over the last two decades, McCormick has succeeded in spending billions for new exhibit halls and meeting space, thereby retaining its title as the biggest. But what has more space actually produced for the center and Chicago?

A 1983 summary of the projected impact of the 1986 North Hall addition noted that the center had attracted 35 convention and tradeshow events with a total attendance of 1,000,000. That sum included 27 of the nation's largest tradeshows (from the *Tradeshow Week 150*, the publication which later became the *Tradeshow Week 200*), which used 7.5 million square feet of exhibit space and attracted 645,485 attendees. The 1983 summary, *Impact in the Chicago and Illinois Economy* (Metropolitan Fair and Exposition Authority, 1983), then estimated that the expansion underway would bring an additional 25 conventions and tradeshows, for a total of 60, with total attendance of 1.5 million.

Now, with major expansions completed in 1986 and 1996, we can evaluate what more exhibit space brought to Chicago. From 27 major tradeshows and about 650,000 attendees before the first expansion, McCormick housed 29 major events in 1989 and 23 in 1990. On average, from 1989 through 1996, the convention center hosted 25 of the major *Tradeshow Week 200* shows. Attendance for these events did increase to about 998,000 per year in 1994, 1995, and 1996. But the center's total convention and tradeshow attendance still fell well below the projected 1.5 million a year. Indeed, a January 1990 study by KPMG Peat Marwick calculated convention and tradeshow attendance for 1989 at 1,016,500–almost exactly the same as in 1983.

If the 1986 expansion appears to have had a far more limited real impact than projected, what about the impact of the more than 800,000 square feet in McCormick South? From 1997 through 2000, the McCormick complex housed just 22 major events on average–a decrease of three from the average before expansion, and five from the 1983 figure. And where major event attendance averaged 997,508 prior to the expansion (from 1989 through 1996), it has since averaged just 937,201 for the years 1997 through 2000. With the model of the ever-growing event space demand in mind, exhibit space use grew from an average of 9.49 million square feet from 1989 through 1996 to 10.13 million from 1997 through 2000–an increase of just 6.75%.

A broader assessment of the 1996 expansion presents a parallel picture. The KPMG Peat Marwick marketing study noted that "demand for exhibit space by tradeshows at McCormick Place and Rosemont O'Hare Expo Center is greater than capacity" and that "interest by events in the middle size event category is strong" (KPMG Peat Marwick, 1990, Sec. IV, p. 7). Thus the essential conclusion of the KPMG analysis was that there was substantial unsatisfied demand for space at McCormick and that an expansion should be quickly filled. The Metropolitan Pier and Exposition Authority even undertook the financing and development of a new 800-room hotel adjacent to the center, with the argument that it was vital to "attract a larger share of the medium and large convention segment of the meetings market" (Metropolitan Pier and Exposition Authority, 1992, p. 35). The overall convention and tradeshow activity at

McCormick averaged 36 events in 1995 and 1996, before the new South Hall opened, with attendance of 1.15 million. From 1997 through 2000, the average event count came to 45 with attendance of 1.29 million. McCormick Place has still not reached the 1.5 million annual convention attendance projected as a result of the 1986 expansion.

The addition of ever more exhibit and meeting space to the nation's largest convention center has certainly not met the promise and forecast of capturing new major events and boosting convention and tradeshow attendance some 50%. In fact, McCormick has actually lost ground in terms of major events and their attendance in recent years. The reality of the national convention marketplace is that it is highly competitive—and growing more so. Orlando seeks to lure events from Chicago, just as Chicago seeks to win them back and add more from Atlanta and elsewhere. Each of these cities can and does add ever more space, on a regular basis, employing the same arguments and rhetoric as Chicago and the state of Illinois.

It is possible to argue that without more space, the center would have performed even more poorly. But McCormick Place boosters always argued that more space would turn into even more—more events, more attendees, more visitor spending, more jobs, more tax revenue. That it clearly did not do. Even in an environment characterized by industry experts and consultants as one of constant regular growth, the nation's largest center, capable of housing the biggest tradeshow and convention events, did not see a real return on its investment of billions of dollars in more space.

Today, with a massive new expansion underway, McCormick Place faces a vastly changed market and travel situation. The combined impact of the economic downturn in 2001 and the events of September 11 affected McCormick's performance as well. The center lost one *Tradeshow Week 200* event from 2000 to 2001, dropping to 20 shows. Exhibit space used fell by 25.5% from a year earlier. But most important, attendance at these major events dropped by 33.4%—to a total of 639,565. That total for 2001 was actually less than the comparable figure for 1983, effectively placing McCormick back where it was two expansions ago.

New Orleans

The Ernest N. Morial Convention Center in New Orleans has been one of the most successful convention facilities in the United States. David Petersen recently described it as capturing "a sizable share of the nationwide convention market," securing for it a position "as one of the most heavily used facilities in the nation" (Petersen, 2001, p. 189). Since its opening in 1984, it has regularly grown in size, hitting a total of 700,000 square feet of exhibition space in 1991 and adding another 400,000 with its Phase III expansion which opened at the beginning of 1999. Building on the attractiveness of New Orleans as a "unique destination," the Morial Center joins Orlando and Las Vegas as locales able to capture a growing fraction of the *Tradeshow Week 200* events during the 1990s.

The expansion of the Morial Center, with about 60% more exhibit space in 1999, provides an effective quasi-experimental test of the impact of added space on an already thriving convention venue. From 1996 through 1998, annual convention and tradeshow delegate attendance averaged 645,550, hitting a total of almost 658,000 for 1998. In a 1994 publication on the center's projected economic impact, the Exhibition Hall Authority projected that Phase III would boost economic impact and tax revenues by some 63% from their 1993 level, gradually increasing further to more than a 70% increase by the year 2000, presumably driven by a parallel boost in attendance (Morial Convention Center, 1994, p. 3).

Delegate attendance did show a dramatic jump in the immediate wake of the expansion opening, reaching 885,997 in 1999–a roughly 35% increase from the previous year (see Figure 7). But for 2000, attendance fell to 731,974. In 2001, with the dual impacts of the economy and September 11, attendance dropped even further to 693,572, or about 5.5% more than before the expansion.

The full story of the Phase III expansion cannot be fully understood until another 2 or 3 years of attendance and performance data can be established. Yet that has not slowed the efforts of the Morial Center to compete by adding even more space. A further expansion is currently underway, designed to add more than 500,000 additional square feet of exhibit space. The latest expansion is not necessarily designed to attract and accommodate the largest conventions and tradeshows, however. The Morial Center is now positioning itself to compete for small to medium size events. According to the feasibility study for the current expansion, the center does not:

> envision single events requiring space in excess of the 1.1 million square feet currently offered at the Morial Center. Rather, the 500,000 to 600,000 square foot addition to the New Orleans convention center inventory will target added multiple events in the 200,000 to 600,000 gross square foot range. (Conventions, Sports and Leisure, 1999b, Executive Summary, p. 6)

The Morial Center thus joins McCormick Place, the Georgia World Congress Center, and a number of other major centers in seeking to fill their newly expanded exhibit space not with the largest events, of which there are only a

FIGURE 7. Morial Convention Center Delegate Attendance by Year

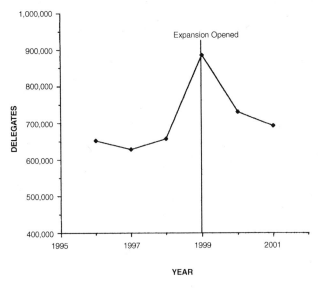

Source: Morial Convention Center management

few, but with multiple small to medium-sized events. New Orleans, Chicago, and Atlanta are thus poised to compete not just among themselves as so-called "Tier 1" destinations, but also with regional competitors. Indeed, the 1999 consultant study on the Morial's expansion argued that:

> Plans are in place, and in some cases construction has started, for expansion to centers in cities such as Nashville, Houston, San Antonio, Denver, and Minneapolis. While these centers will all be smaller than the Morial Center, they have the potential to siphon off smaller and mid-sized events that cannot be held in New Orleans due to lack of space or dates. (Conventions, Sports and Leisure, 1999b, Executive Summary, p. 3)

Baltimore

The Baltimore Convention Center originally opened in 1979, with about 115,000 square feet of exhibit space, as one element of the city's effort to revitalize its core area and reshape the Inner Harbor. One study of urban waterfront development noted in 1983 that the combination of the convention center with the Harborplace retail complex, the National Aquarium, and an adjacent Hyatt hotel offered "a great selling tool in that the hotels, restaurants, shopping, and other attractions are within easy walking distance" (Wrenn, 1983, p. 151).

When Economics Research Associates studied the convention center's performance in late 1992 as part of an assessment of center expansion, they wrote that it "has served the convention and trade show industry well, establishing Baltimore as a desirable destination for the meetings market," having "achieve[d] a relatively strong competitive market standing within the Northeast and Mid-Atlantic region" (Economics Research Associates, 1993, p. 5). The consultant's study indicated that the center had attracted an annual average convention and tradeshow attendance of 176,750 from the mid-1980s through fiscal year 1990/1991. In 1990/1991, that attendance came to 233,461, with 222,905 attendees in fiscal 1991/1992.

But Economics Research Associates foretold difficult times in the years ahead, as new or expanded convention facilities in other competing markets added space, projecting a loss to the state of Maryland each year of more than $136 million in total spending and some 2,697 jobs. But an expansion that roughly doubled the size of the exhibit space would "allow Baltimore to host larger conventions and multiple events during periods of peak demand, minimizing the periods of inactivity at the center and maximizing the potential economic impact" (Economics Research Associates, 1993, p. 5). Economics Research Associates then forecast annual convention and tradeshow attendance for the expanded center of 330,000, with a total count of delegate days reaching 1.163 million.

The expanded Baltimore center opened in April 1997, at a time when the national convention and tradeshow market was commonly described as consistently growing. But the center's attendance for fiscal year 1998 hit just over 227,000 and dropped to 192,625 the following year. Convention and tradeshow attendance was 249,894 in fiscal year 2001, falling to just over 220,000 in fiscal 2002. Clearly, Baltimore's recent performance has fallen far short of the consultant's forecast of 330,000 attendees and has been, in fact, roughly equal to the center's attendance in the early 1990s. More space did not mean more business.

MYTH #5: THE LONG STAYING, BIG SPENDING VISITOR

The rhetoric surrounding convention center development and expansion has long focused on the economic impact presumably derived by communities. As David Petersen has noted, "the primary motive for the development of convention centers is to attract nonresidents whose spending will infuse new money into the economy and create new jobs, increased sales, and more tax revenues" (Petersen, 2001, p. 99). Petersen presents illustrative examples of the overall spending per delegate at international/national/regional conventions ($818.75) and those for state and local meetings ($331.15), noting that the former stay in the convention locale 4.1 days, while state and local attendees have a typical stay of 2.42 days per delegate (Petersen, 2001, p. 101). An empirical survey of convention attendees at the Cincinnati Convention Center concluded that the average total delegate spending at professional association conventions came to $566.91, trade association convention spending was $415.68, and for social, educational, and religious group (SMERF) conventions spending averaged just $171.86 (Price Waterhouse, 1996a, p. 4).

The appeal of attracting out-of-towners who spend generously is obvious. Beyond the impact of their direct spending, there is the multiplied effect of new dollars in the community and the return to the local public sector in tax revenues, from taxes on hotel and motel rooms, to restaurant meals taxes, auto rental taxes, the general sales tax, and the property taxes from new hotels and private developments created as a result of the center. For example, a recent market study for a proposed new convention center in St. Charles, Missouri, a city of 60,000, concluded that it would attract 189,000 attendees by 2008, with about 106,550 non-local residents (C. H. Johnson Consulting, 2002, Sec. 5, p. 6). Those attendees would in turn generate $51.3 million in spending each year, creating 538 new permanent jobs and almost $1 million in annual city tax revenues. A 2002 analysis by KPMG of a new center for Raleigh, North Carolina, concluded that the facility would generate some 900 new jobs in the state and boost convention attendee spending from $21.6 million a year to more than $51.6 million annually.

Promises of broad community-wide economic gain appear again and again in convention center market studies and in the promotion efforts for center bond issues and spending plans. The actual results of a center, however, depend upon its ability to consistently attract visitors who stay and spend. There the reality often falls rather short of the promises and forecasts. Take the case of Boston.

Boston's John B. Hynes Convention Center has long been seen as a highly successful facility in a desirable destination, and its expansion in 1988 "significantly increased the state's share of national and regional convention business" (Petersen, 2001, p. 222). A study of the Hynes' economic impact in 1990 found that it had attracted 335,578 convention and tradeshow attendees, and then estimated, based on national survey data from the International Association of Convention and Visitors Bureaus, that each attendee had spent 4.1 nights in Boston. The result was an estimated total of more than 1.37 million hotel room nights and total direct annual spending of $346.3 million (Bell Associates, 1991).

An estimate of a 4.1 night stay per attendee is not unreasonable in the world of convention center feasibility studies. An analysis of the economic impact of an expanded San Diego Convention Center calculated an average length of stay of 4.2 nights. A 1994 Coopers & Lybrand analysis of an expanded Minneapolis Convention Center calculated an average of 3.38 "delegate days" per attendee. And a January 1990 KPMG Peat Marwick study of Chicago's McCormick Place used an average convention attendee stay of 4.1 days.

Yet when PriceWaterhouseCoopers examined the Hynes' performance in 2002, their figures came out somewhat differently. Data from the Massachusetts Convention Center Authority indicated that the Hynes had generated 334,614 hotel room nights in 1993, falling to 245,719 in 1995, and ultimately reaching 401,367 for 2000. Those are substantial numbers. But they are far from the more than 1.3 million nights claimed for the center in 1990. In fact, relative to the center's convention and tradeshow attendance of 321,350 in 1993, the ratio of room nights to attendance works out to about 1.04 to 1–much less than the 4.1 room night estimate. In fact, based on the data in the PriceWaterhouseCoopers Boston study, from 1993 through 1996, the annual ratio of hotel room nights to attendees works out to an average of 1.03.

These results for Boston, a city commonly viewed as a top visitor destination with a convention center achieving consistently high occupancy, are notable. They suggest that common estimates of average stays of 3 or 4 nights significantly overestimate hotel room use and total spending and provide implausible estimates of what convention centers can actually produce.

Although centers are designed to house events that lure visitors from afar who stay and spend, the actual product of a center will depend upon its mix of events and attendees. Professional association conventions, which typically include seminars and discussion sessions as well as exhibits, are likely to generate longer stays than tradeshows, where the draw is solely exhibits. State and regional association meetings are apt to keep attendees for fewer days than national events, and are more likely to attract local or metropolitan area visitors who choose to drive to the center or use public transportation rather than fly.

Take the case of some individual events housed at McCormick Place in 2000, a recent year unaffected by either economic downturn or terrorism. The January Chicago Gift Show, which used more than 430,000 square feet of exhibit space, attracted 60,000 attendees who used just over 14,000 hotel room nights, for a room night ratio of 0.52. Another major tradeshow event, the National Restaurant Association show, attracted more than 85,000, yet had a room night ratio of only 0.43. For the Chicago Dental Society convention, the ratio came to 0.53. Even a major professional association meeting, the American Dental Association, which garnered Chicago more than 27,700 attendees, generated a room night ratio of just 1.21. During the roughly 49 convention and tradeshow events in 2000, the total of almost 1.44 million attendees used 1.02 million room nights, for a total ratio of 0.71.

With an event mix including a large number of major tradeshows, McCormick Place's capacity to turn attendance into room nights is relatively modest. Yet as Table 6 indicates, even in a number of other prime visitor and convention destination cities, the relationship between attendance and hotel use is far less than an estimate of a consistent 3 or 4 or more night average stay would suggest. For San Francisco's Moscone Center, based on average attendance and average hotel room night use from fiscal 1998 through fiscal 2000, the room night ratio works out to 1.19. For fiscal years 1997 through 2000, the Washington, D.C., Convention Center managed an average room night ratio of 1.07. And for the Baltimore Convention Center, from fiscal year 1998 through 2001, the room night ratio averages to 1.19.

Some convention centers in particularly desirable destinations may fare somewhat better. The San Diego Convention Center reported convention and out-of-town attendance of 346,000 for fiscal 2001, accounting for almost 538,000 hotel room nights, for a room night ratio of 1.55. For fiscal 2002, the room night ratio calculated to 1.65. But while those figures are certainly better than comparable ratios for Boston or Chicago, they are a far cry from an average stay of 4.1 nights.

On the other hand, some convention centers turn in room night ratios that are far smaller than even these. An exhaustive, independent analysis of the impact of Louisville's Kentucky International Convention Center found that in 2001, the room night ratio for conventions and tradeshows came to 0.83. One recent consultant study contained the information that the Fort Worth, Texas,

TABLE 6. Convention Center Attendance and Hotel Room Night Use Cases

City	Time Period	Average Ratio of Room Nights to Attendance
Boston, MA	1993-1996	1.03
Baltimore, MD	FY1 998-2001	1.19
San Diego, CA	FY1 999-2002	1.64
San Francisco, CA	FY1 998-2000	1.19
Washington, DC	FY1 997-2000	1.07
Louisville, KY	1991	0.83
Tucson, AZ	1997-1999	0.70
Fort Worth, TX	1998-2000	0.67
Chicago, IL	1998-2000	0.64

Source: Center feasibility studies and annual reports.

Convention Center averaged an annual convention and tradeshow attendance of 142,945 from 1998 through 2000 (C. H. Johnson, 2001, Sec. 3, p. 6). For that same period, hotel room night use by conventions and tradeshows averaged 95,400–a room night ratio of 0.67.

A number of people obviously attend convention events in Fort Worth or Chicago or Boston in a given year. Their use of hotel rooms, and their spending, can constitute a substantial economic impact. But the evidence across a range of major convention centers suggests that simply multiplying total annual attendance by an assumed stay of 4, 3, or even 2 nights leads to a dramatic overstatement of that economic impact. A great many attendees may "day trip," simply driving to the convention or tradeshow for the day and spending for a meal and parking. Others who do stay overnight may double or even triple up in a hotel room, with the obvious consequence of far lower average spending. With room night ratios of around 1.0 clearly quite common even for prime destinations, the promises of most center feasibility and market studies appear quite hollow. In turn, the economic import of a new or expanded convention center, even where it can draw substantial new attendance, will be far more limited than commonly argued and publicly assumed. As a major investment of public dollars intended to serve a broader economic development purpose, the worth of any given convention center project is open to serious question.

MYTH #6: THE NEED FOR A HEADQUARTERS HOTEL

Recent years have seen an explosion in the development of publicly-subsidized and even publicly-owned hotels designed to help convention centers compete for business. Hotels built with substantial public financial assistance include the Indianapolis, Philadelphia, and Baltimore Marriotts, a new Westin in Charlotte, North Carolina, and Tampa's Marriott Waterfront. The Hyatt McCormick Place in Chicago is owned by the Metropolitan Pier and Exposition Authority, which owns McCormick Place. And public nonprofit corporations own an 800 room Hilton being built in Austin, Texas, and a 1,200-room Hilton in downtown Houston.

The boom in new headquarters hotels in part reflects the risk associated with what used to be the private investment "induced" by convention center development. Where the private market was once willing to provide the investment capital for major downtown hotel developments, today's major convention-oriented hotel carries too great a risk. Thus even with the promise of some $13 million in public assistance, the Starwood Corporation and The Related Companies consumed more than 5 years in attempting to secure the equity and debt financing for a new 1,200-room Sheraton hotel adjacent to San Antonio's recently expanded Henry B. Gonzalez Convention Center, only to fail in early 2002.

The result has become an increasing turn to public investment and outright ownership, either directly by a city government or through a shell nonprofit corporation. The name on the front of a hotel may be a familiar "Hilton" or "Hyatt," yet, increasingly, the dollars and the risk-taking behind that hotel are local governments', with cases like Sacramento's Grand Sheraton, Fort Worth's planned Hilton, and the Radisson in Myrtle Beach, South Carolina.

The willingness of local government to invest in new hotels also reflects the combination of a belief in the economic power of the convention business and the argument by industry consultants that a headquarters hotel is vital to a city's competitive position. Thus, in a 1996 assessment of the performance of the Charlotte Convention Center, C. H. Johnson noted that "the Charlotte Convention Center has fewer events and lower average attendance than the other four cities [Baltimore, Denver, Indianapolis, and Minneapolis] compared in this analysis," and "Charlotte's exhibit hall occupancy is also lower than the comparable cities" (C. H. Johnson, 1996, Sec. 4, p. 4). The Johnson study went on to propose a set of public initiatives to improve the city's convention "package." That list included the development of a major retail and entertainment complex as "the most fundamental initiative the Greater Charlotte area could embrace" (C. H. Johnson, 1996, Sec. 6, p. 5). But the consultant also called for the development of up to 1,500 new hotel rooms in the area of the convention center by the year 2000.

One year later, in July 1997, Johnson Consulting examined the convention prospects of Austin, Texas. While the Johnson analysis called for the expansion of the convention center by a minimum of 130,000 square feet of exhibit space, it also expressed strong concern over the city's downtown hotel supply. Noting that the lack of a convention-oriented hotel room supply "will become more detrimental under a Convention Center expansion scenario," the consultant argued that "without a concentrated effort by the City to influence and control hotel development, the CBD [Central Business District] will lose an opportunity to leverage the Convention Center's impact" (C. H. Johnson, 1997, Sec. 3, pp. 12-13). The Johnson study recommended a combination of public initiatives, including tax rebates and even direct ownership, as "necessary in Austin in order to steer development toward the area where it can best benefit the Center and City" (C. H. Johnson, 1997, Sec. 3, pp. 24-25).

A host of other studies also argue the need for a headquarters hotel as a necessary adjunct of convention center development. The analysis of Albany, New York's, convention prospects by the Strategic Advisory Group recommended that a 400-room hotel attached to the proposed new convention center was vital, and that "the closer the proximity of the hotel to the convention center, the greater the center's potential for success" (Strategic Advisory Group, 2001b, p. 2). And a July 2002 study of convention center expansion in Raleigh, North Carolina, by KPMG found that "a new convention quality headquarters hotel that offers approximately 400 to 500 rooms within walking distance to the new or expanded facility would likely be required in order to increase the proposed new facility's competitiveness" (KPMG, 2002, p. 10).

While the call for a headquarters hotel as an essential requirement for a successful, competitive center has become quite common, there has been almost no research on the role or import of such a hotel. Feasibility studies commonly cite survey results from meeting planners to argue for such investment. The Strategic Advisory Group (2002) has argued that a survey of meeting planners regarding their interest in the new Boston Convention and Exhibition Center demonstrated the merit of a hotel. The results of the survey showed that while only 26% of the 100 top meeting planners indicated a willingness to use the new center with a 400-room hotel adjacent, the level of interest rose to 85% with a 1,200-room hotel. Still, a statement of interest on the part of a planner in an unfinished center is a relatively modest substantive justification as it carries no cost or real commitment.

Perhaps the most substantial case for the role of a headquarters hotel has been made by Karen E. Rubin, a vice president of the consulting firm HVS International. Noting that hotels are themselves visitor and dollar generators, Rubin argues that local governments now view hotels as a means of generating additional public tax revenues. After stating that "an oft-cited reason for underperforming civic conference and convention centers is a dearth of hotels rooms," Rubin documents the case of the new Pennsylvania Convention Center in Philadelphia and its adjacent Marriott hotel:

> where new hotel rooms really were needed to permit the convention center to reach its potential. . . . When the 1,200 room Marriott opened in 1995, the new rooms represented a substantial addition to supply; about 16% to the total Philadelphia market supply. . . . In this case, the new hotel rooms were to the market what gasoline is to an engine: you need it to make it go. In the positive economic conditions of the middle and late 1990s, Philadelphia-like stories are occurring more and more. (Rubin, 2000, p. 6)

The Philadelphia case would appear to support the notion that a major new hotel serves to boost the competitive prospects of a convention center, "making it go." The empirical issue is thus the impact of the hotel on the convention center's performance, not the performance and success of the headquarters hotel itself.

The Pennsylvania Convention Center hosted 42 conventions and tradeshows in 1995, the year the Marriott opened, with a total attendance of 195,795. The next year, the event count reached 48 and attendance hit 318,737, then rose to 354,300 for 1997. Yet, since 1997, attendance has dropped: 204,355 in 1999, 238,308 in 2000 (including the Republican National Convention with 30,000 attendees), and, ultimately, to 46 events and 199,000 attendees in 2001.

If, as Rubin argues, the Marriott headquarters hotel is the gasoline that makes the convention center engine go, the center would appear to be in serious need of a tune up. To the extent that the development of the Marriott made some difference in the overall appeal and performance of the Pennsylvania Convention Center, that appeal proved quite short-lived. A 1988 feasibility and market study for the center predicted that its convention and tradeshow attendance would grow each year after opening, reaching 333,000 by 2000 and 346,000 by 2001. Recently, even with the presumed boost from the Marriott, it has steadily lost attendance and fallen well short of the forecast.

A parallel case of a city with an existing headquarters hotel is San Antonio, Texas. The city's Henry B. Gonzalez Convention Center is served by some 3,500 nearby hotel rooms, including the 1,000-room Marriott Rivercenter, opened in 1988, about one block from the center and the 500-room Marriott Riverwalk directly across the street from the center. Marriott manages and books the two together as the primary headquarters hotels.

The San Antonio Convention and Visitors Bureau has collected consistent data on attendance and room night activity for the Gonzalez Center since 1993, after the opening of the Marriott Rivercenter. Although the time span does not allow for a full before and after comparison, it does provide some indication of the continuing impact of large headquarters hotel on ongoing center performance.

The annual attendance for the Gonzalez Center is shown in Figure 8. The center regularly managed convention and tradeshow attendance of about 575,000 through the mid-1990s, hitting a peak of almost 608,000 in 1998. Since that time, and before the impacts of 2001, attendance declined to about 515,500 in 2000. The 2001 attendance figure was 524,743. A companion chart of hotel room night activity at the center is shown in Figure 9. While the center managed a peak of about 1.04 million room nights in 1998, its subsequent hotel use impact has fallen to about 921,500 in 2000 and 903,000 for 2001.

After the completion of an expansion which doubled the center's exhibit space in 2001, San Antonio may experience some increase in convention activity in future years. But it is clear that the mere presence of a major conven-

FIGURE 8. Henry B. Gonzalez Convention Center Attendance by Year

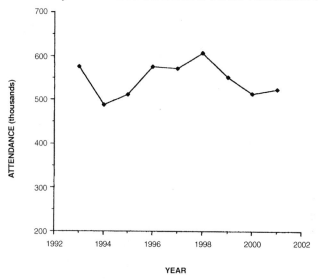

Source: PKF, Market Study: San Antonio Convention Hotel

FIGURE 9. Henry B. Gonzalez Convention Center Room Nights by Year

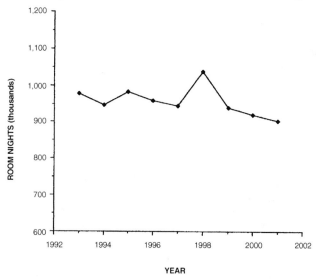

Source: PKF, Market Study: San Antonio Convention Hotel

tion headquarters hotel does not in and of itself suffice to maintain attendance or room night activity levels over time, even in a market described as consistently growing.

Another recent case of a headquarters hotel specifically intended to boost the activity levels and performance of a new convention center is Sacramento, California, a city which spurred the current boom in publicly-developed hotels. The city expanded its convention center in March 1996 to a total of 134,000 square feet of exhibition space. Yet even with an expanded and renovated center, the city and its consultant recognized a need for an additional supply of hotel rooms. When a number of private hotel development initiatives failed, the city chose to develop the hotel itself. The city created a financing authority and a hotel corporation to own and operate a 500-room hotel under the Sheraton flag, at a cost of more than $104 million, backed by the revenues from the hotel and an adjacent garage. The city's consultant projected that the new hotel would add about 60,000 annual hotel room nights to the center's overall performance by fiscal year 2005, bringing it to a total of 206,736 room nights generated.

The new Sheraton Grand Sacramento opened at the end of April 2001, and quite quickly faced a highly competitive environment significantly affected by the events of September 11. For the first three quarters of 2002, the hotel succeeded in averaging an occupancy rate of 67.3% with an average daily room rate of $124.51. The performance of the hotel itself is thus only slightly less than its original projections. At the same time, the new Sheraton also appears to have had a clear negative impact on other competing downtown hotels. The Hyatt, Holiday Inn, Doubletree, and Hilton each saw both their occupancy rate and average daily room rate drop from 2001–in one case a drop of $20.00 in average rate as well as a decrease in occupancy from 78.1% to 74.3%–as the Sheraton's occupancy rate rose (PKF, 2002b).

The more central question is the impact of the hotel on the performance of the Sacramento Convention Center. Given the hotel's opening date, its impact should be clearly seen in fiscal year 2002, which began June 1, 2001.

From fiscal year 1997 through fiscal 2000, the center averaged convention and tradeshow attendance of 138,833, rising to 212,651 for fiscal 2001–effectively prior to the impact of the Sheraton Grand. For fiscal 2002, the center's attendance, obviously affected by the overall travel downturn, fell to 172,215. Estimated attendance for 2002/2003, based on bookings, comes to 172,575, with a total of 99,686 hotel room nights booked (see Table 7).

These data on convention attendance and room night bookings suggest that the hotel's impact on the convention center may have been to stabilize attendance, albeit with a drop from fiscal 2001 (pre-hotel) to fiscal 2002. Hotel room night use shows a modest increase of about 20,000 annual nights. While

TABLE 7. Sacramento Convention Center Convention Bookings

Fiscal Year (ends June 30)	Meetings	Delegates	Room Nights
1996-97	60	133,050	61,247
1997-98	49	131,700	58,847
1998-99	58	154,495	79,588
1999-00	60	136,085	86,980
2000-01	53	212,651	82,609
2001-02 Hotel Opens 5/01	68	172,215	103,584
2002-03 estimated	53	172,575	99,686

Source: Sacramento Convention and Visitors Bureau.

the city's commitment to a headquarters hotel may have provided an additional increment of convention-related room nights to the center, it certainly has not had a dramatic impact to date. That conclusion is supported by the decreasing room rates and occupancy for other competitive downtown hotels. The convention market has not grown enough to support the Sheraton and its competitors.

Even these changes in center performance may not necessarily reflect solely the presence of the new hotel. At the time the hotel was developed, the Sacramento Convention and Visitors Bureau implemented new marketing and booking criteria, designed to assist "the maximum production of hotel room nights" (Sacramento City Financing Authority, 1999, p. 73). The Sacramento CVB offered events booking a minimum of 1,000 hotel rooms on two nights a deal: they will be "granted meeting space proportional to hotel room usage for up to four events days at no charge . . . allow[ing] the Convention Center to reward those events that utilize a greater number of hotel rooms by reducing convention space costs" (Sacramento City Financing Authority, 1999, p. 73). A parallel, if less generous, offer is available for events using more than 525 rooms on two nights. By discounting center space down to zero cost, Sacramento has been able to offer a potent incentive to meeting planners beyond the supply of new hotel rooms.

If the Sacramento case, together with the experience in Philadelphia and San Antonio, fails to provide compelling evidence of the impact of a headquarters hotel, it does neatly illustrate the lengths to which local government is willing to go to spur convention activity and visitor volume. Public investment in a hotel is likely to be followed by aggressive marketing efforts, space discounts, and a host of other inducements. And if one headquarters hotel fails to generate a business or economic impact deemed sufficient, it will likely be followed by another publicly-aided or built hotel (as proposed in San Antonio) or a proposal for a new arena (as in Los Angeles) or a call for a new light rail line connecting the convention center and hotel to centers of entertainment and activity downtown (as in Charlotte).

THE NEW MARKET

The convention center boom of recent years has been built on a foundation of voluminous consultant reports and abundant political rhetoric, swathed in a grand set of myths about growth, demand, economic impact, and competition. Amidst a great deal of mythology, what is clear is that a great deal of new exhibit space in the form of entirely new or greatly expanded convention centers has recently arrived on the market, and far more is due. Although *Tradeshow Week* recently counted some 12.2 million square feet of space due to be added over the next few years, that sum does not include possible additions in a host of new cities armed with favorable, indeed enthusiastic, feasibility studies. The list of new cities includes some noted here, such as Albany, New York, and Schaumburg, Illinois, as well as St. Charles, Missouri; Santa Fe, New Mexico; Arlington, Virginia; Arlington, Texas; Augusta, Georgia; Lancaster, Pennsylvania; Mattoon, Illinois; Oshkosh, Wisconsin; Lombard, Illinois; and Branson, Missouri.

Even with the shifts in travel and convention activity over the last two years, cities continue to perceive and promote convention center development as an all but certain economic development strategy. Visitor spending can and does sustain a part of a local economy, particularly in diverse destinations. Yet it is clear that each and every one of these communities faces a difficult competitive future, despite their obvious hometown boosterism and enthusiasm.

Perhaps the most remarkable feature of the current rush to convention center development is its convergence on the small to medium-sized event market. Smaller cities like Lancaster and St. Charles tout their advantages, particularly for modestly sized state and regional groups and events. At the same time, the largest centers in the nation justify their own expansions with the argument that it is the middle of the meetings market that offers the most promising target and that they can and should serve simultaneous multiple events. Thus the Morial Center in New Orleans is armed with arguments that it is competing against an expanded center in San Antonio, while Fort Worth has a set of consultant studies that call for it to compete for state and regional events with San Antonio and Austin, and San Antonio now has a feasibility study that contends that its competition is Austin, New Orleans, Las Vegas, and Orlando. And of course, each of those centers is also expanding—all aiming at the same set of events.

THE FUTURE IS HERE

The last two years have witnessed some clear changes in the shape and direction of the convention and tradeshow industry. Where once it was easy to argue that the industry was effectively recession-proof and growth was both persistent and inevitable, that conclusion now has far less empirical support. Nonetheless, the weight of consultant studies and optimistic industry growth forecasts continues to grow. The result is a steady pace of new convention center and expansion projects that promise a continuing flow of exhibit space—in major centers like Las Vegas and Chicago, in mid-sized centers like Dallas and Cleveland, and in a host of smaller cities and suburbs that each see their economic fortunes in the meetings industry.

The question of what might happen if and when a glut of space occurs is easily answered: it is happening now. Charlotte, North Carolina, has offered "convention gold" in an advertisement in a major industry publication, promising free center rental or funding for speakers, shuttle buses, or food service. Austin, Texas, has a website that offers meeting planners a "bonus" of free facility rental, free reception, or free entertainment. Sacramento plugs its appeal with free convention center rent. Los Angeles offers the same. Boston, in an effort to fill the new Boston Convention and Exhibition Center, offered the Macworld Expo free center rent, free use of city facilities, discounts on exhibitor services and transportation, and a guaranteed supply of reduced cost hotel rooms. And the CEO of the San Diego Convention Center Corporation has noted that even that prime destination has been obliged to offer exhibition space at reduced rates and discounts on local hotel rooms.

For meeting planners and tradeshow organizers, it's sale time—the natural response to an imbalance between supply and demand. And when things go on sale, everyone has to compete harder. The Macworld event that Boston succeeded in luring came from a run in New York. Now, the Javits Center in New York is seeking to compete for its replacement and other events, and New York City convention and hospitality officials argue that the 814,400 square foot Javits Center is too small. What New York City ostensibly needs to compete is an expanded convention center.

For center users, sale time means markdowns on center space, bargains on catering and shuttle buses, and convention centers working overtime to add space, build headquarters hotels, and boost amenities. The result is a dynamic where planners appear to have shortened their booking times, seeking ever-better deals and discounts. At the same time, convention centers and convention and visitors bureaus are coming under increasing scrutiny and questioning, as traditional marketing approaches have decreasing success even in the most desirable markets.

The convergence of a flat convention and tradeshow market with the addition of millions of square feet of new exhibition space does not bode well for the future. It is, of course, possible that an imbalance between supply and demand will be self-correcting. As cities see a more difficult situation ahead, they might be dissuaded from adding more space or reach the conclusion that the convention market offers too little opportunity for advantage and local economic development.

Yet, in the wake of September 11, few cities appear willing to abandon or even defer their expansion and development plans. Recent months have seen a host of new plans for convention center development, including bond and spending proposals on the ballot in Kansas City, Phoenix, and San Jose, as well as forward movement on new headquarters hotel efforts in Fort Worth, Dallas, San Antonio, Washington, Baltimore, Boston, Denver, and Pittsburgh. The quest for more space by no means appears over.

The reality of the world of convention center development is that there is no effective local correction mechanism—no means by which the failure, or even modest results, of convention center development force a city to re-examine its plans and policy choices. The bonds that back convention center development are most commonly repaid by broadly based revenue streams, including taxes on all city or county hotel rooms, auto rental taxes, restaurant taxes, and even general sales taxes. Whether people come to the convention center or not, the bondholders are repaid. Once, the debt that built or expanded a convention center had to be approved by the voters. That remains the case in a small number of cities, including California cities still limited by the fiscal structure imposed by Proposition 13. But increasingly, convention center debt can be issued without any sort of public referendum, thus insulating this form of major public investment from the voters and their potential wrath or alternative investment preferences.

At the same time, local governments are playing an increasingly limited role in convention center finance. With the argument that many of the fiscal benefits from convention goers and their spending are captured by state government, a number of cities have succeeded in winning state grants and fiscal support for convention center development. In places like Seattle, Hartford, Providence, and Philadelphia, the state government has become the convention center builder and booster. Indeed, a proposal for financing an expanded convention center in Phoenix calls for the state of Arizona to spend its dollars roughly proportional to the anticipated increase in state revenues. Thus, a convention center justified by a consultant's feasibility study becomes the beneficiary of the fictive state revenues from the attendees who are projected to come.

Every community appears to believe that its downtown and its attractions offer the unique combination that will appeal to dozens of meeting planners and thousands of convention and tradeshow attendees, even if they haven't come in years past. Much like the cities of the 1950s and 1960s that embarked on ambitious urban renewal clearance programs only to find that there was no market for the land, and the cities of the 1970s and 1980s that embarked on expansive urban retail and festival marketplace developments only to find them white elephants, the investment in conventions and visitors is remarkably free from any serious analysis or public review. In this environment–with public officials who seem to believe that each consultant study is uniquely relevant to their situation and every meeting planner is waiting to come if only there were more space, or a bigger hotel, or some other lure–the investment in convention centers can only grow, regardless of demand, until the next grand solution for urban ills emerges.

REFERENCES

Bell Associates. (1991). *John B. Hynes Veterans Memorial Convention Center 1990 Economic Impact Report*. Cambridge, MA: Author.

C. H. Johnson Consulting. (1996). *City of Charlotte convention center maximization study*. Chicago: Author.

C. H. Johnson Consulting. (1997). *A strategic plan for Austin's convention center industry: Final report*. Chicago: Author.

C. H. Johnson Consulting. (2001). *Fort Worth Convention Center headquarters hotel analysis*. Chicago: Author.

C. H. Johnson Consulting. (2002). *Report to the St. Charles County Convention and Sports Facilities Authority: Convention center feasibility*. Chicago: Author.

Center for Exhibition Industry Research. (1998). *Size of the exhibition industry*. Bethesda, MD: Author.

Center for Exhibition Industry Research. (2002, September). *The exhibition industry situation analysis*. Chicago: Author.

Conventions, Sports and Leisure. (1999a). *Analysis of the long term convention facility needs for the Nashville market*. Minneapolis, MN: Author.

Conventions, Sports and Leisure. (1999b). *Long range market demand and feasibility analysis for Ernest N. Morial New Orleans Exhibition Hall Authority*. Minneapolis, MN: Author.

Conventions, Sports and Leisure. (2002). *Market analysis: Cincinnati Convention Center expansion*. Minneapolis, MN: Author.

Coopers & Lybrand. (1993). *Commonwealth of Massachusetts megaplex, convention center, and stadium feasibility analysis*. Dallas, TX: Author.

Coopers & Lybrand. (1994). *Market, financial and economic impact analysis for the proposed expansion of the Minneapolis Convention Center.* Dallas, TX: Author.

Coopers & Lybrand. (1996). *An analysis of Fort Worth public assembly facilities.* Dallas, TX: Author.

Coopers & Lybrand. (1997a). *Analysis for the proposed Washington Convention Center.* Dallas, TX: Author.

Coopers & Lybrand. (1997b). *A market, building program, financial operations and economic impact analysis for potential expansion of the Jacob K. Javits Convention Center of New York.* Dallas, TX: Author.

Deloitte and Touche. (1993). *Financial feasibility study of a new convention center in the District of Columbia.* Washington, D.C.: Author.

Dodds, A. (2002, May 6). Rate of decline eases for first quarter tradeshows. *Tradeshow Week,* p. 1.

Economics Research Associates. (1993). *Expansion feasibility update for Baltimore Convention Center.* Los Angeles: Author.

Garvin, A. (2002). *The American city: What works, what doesn't, second edition.* New York: McGraw Hill.

KPMG Peat Marwick. (1990). *Metropolitan Pier and Exposition Authority long range marketing study.* Chicago: Author.

KPMG. (1998). *Rio Salado Crossing: Market, financial, and economic fiscal impact analysis related to the proposed Arizona Exposition and Convention Center.* Tampa, FL: Author.

KPMG. (2002). *Market and financial analysis for the additional convention center space in Raleigh, North Carolina.* Tampa, FL: Author.

Meetings and Conventions. (2002). *Meetings market report.* Secaucus, NJ: Author.

Metropolitan Fair and Exposition Authority. (1983). *Impact in the Chicago and Illinois Economy.* Chicago: Author.

Metropolitan Pier and Exposition Authority. (1992). *$868,849,764.60 McCormick Place expansion project bonds.* Chicago: Author.

Morial Convention Center. (1994). *Economic impact: Current and projected with phase III expansion.* New Orleans: Author.

Pannell Kerr Foster. (1988). *Market demand and economic impact study for the proposed Pennsylvania Convention Center.* Philadelphia: Author.

Petersen, D. (2001). *Developing sports, convention, and performing arts centers* (3rd ed.). Washington, D.C.: Urban Land Institute.

PKF. (2002). *Market study with prospective financial analysis: Proposed 1,500-room headquarters convention center hotel, San Antonio, Texas.* Houston, TX: Author.

PKF. (2003). *Sacramento Grand, Sacramento: Third quarter market and operational analysis 2002.* Sacramento, CA: Author.

Price Waterhouse. (1991). *San Diego Convention Center: Market, financial and economic impact analysis.* Tampa, FL: Author.

Price Waterhouse. (1993). *Expansion of Boston's convention center facilities, final report, phase I.* Tampa, FL: Author.

Price Waterhouse. (1996a). *Cincinnati Convention Center survey.* Tampa, FL: Author.

Price Waterhouse. (1996b). *Georgia World Congress Center: Market, economic & fiscal impact analysis of proposed phase IV expansion.* Tampa, FL: Author.

PriceWaterhouseCoopers. (1999). *Cincinnati Convention Center expansion study: Final draft.* Tampa, FL: Author.

PriceWaterhouseCoopers. (2001). *Cleveland convention center & headquarter hotel analysis.* Tampa, FL: Author.

PriceWaterhouseCoopers. (2002). Boston Convention and Exhibition Center marketing study. Tampa, FL: Author.

Roberts, T. (2002, June 12). Higher hotel tax urged. *Silicon Valley/San Jose Business Journal.* Retrieved March 12, 2003, from http://sanjose.bizjournals.com/sanjose/stories/2002/06/10/daily49.html

Rubin, K. (2000, Spring). What can make new hotel construction economically feasible when new hotel construction isn't economically feasible? *Real Estate Issues,* pp. 1-6.

Sacramento City Financing Authority. (1999). *$92,800,000 Senior revenue bond (Sacramento convention center hotel project).* Sacramento, CA: Author.

Stein and Company. (1995). *Market and financial analysis: Austin's convention and performing arts facilities.* Chicago: Author.

Stein and Company. (1996). *Financial feasibility study prepared for Wisconsin Center District.* Chicago: Author.

Strategic Advisory Group. (2001a). *Schaumburg Convention Center and Entertainment Complex feasibility study.* Duluth, GA: Author.

Strategic Advisory Group. (2001b). *City of Albany, Department of Development and Planning, convention center market and economic impact analysis.* Duluth, GA: Author.

Strategic Advisory Group. (2002). Hotel public-private partnerships: Changing the paradigm. Retrieved March 12, 2003, from http://www.strategicadvisorygroup.net/Newsletter3.pdf

Tradeshow Week. (2002a). *Major Exhibit Hall Directory.* Los Angeles: Author.

Tradeshow Week. (2002b). *Tradeshow Week 200.* Los Angeles: Author.

Tradeshow Week. (2002c). *Tradeshow Week Data Book.* Los Angeles: Author.

U. S. Bureau of the Census. (2002). *Annual value of state and local construction* (C30 series). Washington, DC: Author.

Wrenn, D. (1983). *Urban waterfront development.* Washington, D.C.: Urban Land Institute.

The City as a Destination: Measuring Its Attractiveness

David C. Petersen, BA

SUMMARY. The findings of this original research provide a methodology that eliminates the subjectivity inherent in prior methods utilized to rank or gauge the capability of a city to attract delegates to conventions of professional associations. These new analytical techniques may also be employed to estimate convention attendee market shares, as well as determine reliable rankings of a destination's "attractiveness" and its financial or economic sustainability. The criteria identified in this study also comprise the "vital signs" for measuring a city's future health. *[Article copies available for a fee from The Haworth Document Delivery Service: 1-800-HAWORTH. E-mail address: <docdelivery@haworthpress.com> Website: <http://www.HaworthPress. com> © 2004 by The Haworth Press, Inc. All rights reserved.]*

KEYWORDS. Convention centers, economic sustainability, "Mix-Mass-Mesh," vital signs, center city, real estate investment

Ranking the attractiveness of a visitor destination or a city seems as popular as the chant "We're #1." Even when we ask an association exec to explain

---

David C. Petersen is President of Town Planning Research (TPR).

Address correspondence to: David C. Petersen, Town Planning Research, 55 Highfield Way, Whangarei, New Zealand (E-mail: TownPlan@Clear.Net.NZ).

[Haworth co-indexing entry note]: "The City as a Destination: Measuring Its Attractiveness." Petersen, David C.. Co-published simultaneously in *Journal of Convention & Event Tourism* (The Haworth Hospitality Press, an imprint of The Haworth Press, Inc.) Vol. 6, No. 1/2, 2004, pp. 145-157; and: *Current Issues in Convention and Exhibition Facility Development* (ed: Robert R. Nelson) The Haworth Hospitality Press, an imprint of The Haworth Press, Inc., 2004, pp. 145-157. Single or multiple copies of this article are available for a fee from The Haworth Document Delivery Service [1-800-HAWORTH, 9:00 a.m. - 5:00 p.m. (EST). E-mail address: docdelivery@haworthpress.com].

http://www.haworthpress.com/web/JCET
Digital Object Identifier: 10.1300/J452v06n01_08

their organization's reason for selecting a city to host their next convention, we more than likely will receive their "opinions" rather than their actual motives. (The only truly credible response the author has heard is "Because we get higher attendance in City X.") Due to the unreliability, subjectivity, and fraudulent (shameful) practices utilized to rank or measure the "attractiveness" of a city, the author has been driven (perhaps even obsessed) to identify reliable and predictive methods. These new empirical methods objectively and scientifically gauge a city's ability to attract conventions. They also assess the city's ability to attract private investment in new development.

Most important, this new method measures the long-term capability of a city to attract the capital needed for its future renewal and renovation; that is, its survival. This "capital-attracting" capability may be referred to as the city's economic sustainability or its intrinsic capacity for self-perpetuation. It always produces a very pleasing exhilaration (for the author) to learn about the reconstruction of a venue such as Gran Teatre del Liceau (the Opera House) in center city Barcelona or the renovation of Radio City Music Hall in Manhattan; to read about the ever-increasing values of real estate in the thousand-year-old cities of Prague or Budapest, the continuing enhancement of property values in "Old Hyde Park Village" in Tampa, or the continuing prosperity of the town of Marimont, outside Cincinnati, Ohio. The sad truth is, when cities fail to attract new capital investment, or large numbers of convention attendees, they are in the process of dying–in the jaws of death–if not already dead.

The primary determinants of visitor spending (total attendance, length of stay, and spending per delegate) are always maximized when associations select venues in city centers that everyone enjoys visiting just because they are fun. San Francisco, Boston, Seattle, and Chicago continue to rank highest in professional association attendance and spending per attendee. Based on the data collected in surveys for the "Convention Industry Report" (initiated by the author in 1986), center city convention centers enjoying the highest attendance in each of the annual reporting periods over the 13 years beginning in 1986 and ending in 1999 were New York, Chicago, Washington, D.C., San Francisco, Boston, Atlanta, Seattle, Philadelphia, and San Diego (Petersen, 1985-1999). Most of these cities are also in the "Top 10" cities in terms of the number of hotel rooms within walking distance (six blocks) of its convention center. Whereas 25% to 40% of the occupancy in a full-service hotel is generated by conventions or "group" business, it is axiomatic that center cities with the highest concentrations of hotel rooms would also enjoy the highest levels of convention attendees. This applies whether the meeting of a professional association is hosted in a large convention hotel or in a convention center. It is also axiomatic that spending by delegates to meetings held in cities with unique retail stores proximate to the convention center or headquarters hotel is many times higher than spending in cities where the retail outlets are more "generic" or remote ($100 per delegate vs. $15 per delegate) (International Association of Convention and Visitor Bureaus, 1980).

INTRODUCTION

References to tourist or visitor destinations usually conjure up images of locations offering theme parks, golf resorts, casino gaming, or other unique recreational or entertainment attractions. While these images may be the most common that are called to mind, the largest daily spending per visitor is generated by attendees to conventions, conferences, and meetings of professional associations: bankers, scientists, engineers, and others. The majority of these types of events, and the largest assemblies of visitors to these events, occur in our city centers, the downtown districts of our largest metro areas.

Whether your city is among the largest or not so large, a "gateway" or a regional city, its downtown (or uptown) convention center and hotels serve as the primary locations for the annual meetings or conventions of professional associations.

Cities are selected for these events based on their attractiveness. From year to year, these meetings attract larger or fewer attendees depending upon the attractiveness of the location or destination selected for the meeting. The amount of money spent by each attendee, the number of accompanying persons, or party-size, and their length of stay (total room-nights generated) will depend upon the attractiveness of the location.

Clearly, the attractiveness of the destination is the single most important factor in maximizing the economic benefits created from the non-resident spending by convention attendees. We all can readily identify meetings we've attended at popular destinations, albeit in substandard venues, that attracted larger attendance than meetings held in "state-of-the-art" convention centers located in less popular destinations.

Not so clearly, the term "attractiveness" sounds very subjective and the ranking of cities according to their attractiveness *is* highly vulnerable to manipulation. This ranking or measuring may be manipulated by opting to include or exclude any criterion that may combine to create the (pre-determined) desired result. Such scores or rankings may be published in the *Places Rated Almanac* or chosen as the "factoid"-of-the-day in *USA Today* or they could be masqueraded as the "objective" findings of an international consulting firm. But a careful reading of the methodology employed to calculate these rankings will reveal the great extent to which they are totally reliant on the specific criteria selected by the firm or staff (often based on opinion surveys, popularity contests, or "intuitive" judgments) and the weighting given to each criterion.

The findings of the author's original research offer a methodology that eliminates the subjectivity of prior methods. These new analytical techniques may be employed to plan the revitalization of a center city or estimate convention attendee market shares, as well as determine reliable rankings, performance scores, and provide the "vital signs" for measuring a city's future financial health or its economic sustainability.

Each center city's relative attractiveness, "magnetism," or "drawing power," its ability to capture conventions or new capital investment is calculated by (a) determining the mix of specific types of building space or activities (for example, office, retail, residential) in the center city; (b) quantifying the magnitude or critical mass of those various building types or activities (total occupied office space, volume of retail sales, size of residential population, and so forth); and (c) measuring the proximity, or mesh, of these activities or occupied commercial and residential buildings to each other; in other words, the inter-activity of center city residents, workers, and visitors. These critical characteristics or vital signs are defined by the author as the "Mix-Mass-Mesh" of the center city.

The relative financial success of a center city is verified by its capture of new investment from year to year (just as its performance as a visitor destination is determined by its annual convention attendance or total annual convention attendee/visitor-days). This is its relative "ranking" compared to other cities as measured by the total new capital invested by the nation's largest real estate investors, lenders, and developers.

Evidence from empirical research demonstrates these same relationships also predict success for cities in European and Asia Pacific regions as well. Total attendance to conventions (or congresses as they are called in Europe) is directly related to the center city's total hotel rooms supply, occupied "class A" office space, and residential population.

The author believes this same required "Mix-Mass-Mesh" may be considered a prerequisite, or a "law," that determines the financial success or the attractiveness of not just center cities, but also of neighborhoods, entire communities, and other types of large-scale pedestrian-oriented real estate development. Other types of large scale developments would include convention centers; mixed-use commercial developments; residential buildings; performing arts centers; festive retail or "urban entertainment" centers; and other commercial, civic, and cultural developments.

Americans have enthusiastically been attracted to the intimacy, diversity, and vitality of European cities. Whether we are compelled to "measure" their vital signs or just enjoy the ambiance, we can be assured they are wonderful places to live, to work, and to attend a convention. In other words, because they possess the "Mix-Mass-Mesh."

Although cities like Las Vegas and Orlando certainly rank among the top U.S. convention destinations, these are predominantly conventions of trade associations or trade shows. When compared to professional associations delegates, visitors to the large-scale exhibitions of trade associations spend less per day, have a shorter length of stay, with fewer "accompanying others" (smaller party size), and are less inclined to pre- or post-event visitation.

The Las Vegas Convention Center and the concentration of its hotel rooms are not located in the downtown or center city. The same is true of Orlando's convention center and hotel rooms. While the Las Vegas Convention Center is located near the concentration of its full-service casino hotels on "The Strip," south of its downtown, Orlando's convention center is located in the Walt Disney World resort area, approximately 15 miles southwest of the center city. The extraordinarily large convention delegate attendance achieved by these destinations is attributable to the extraordinarily large concentrations of their hotel rooms (the largest supply of rooms in the world) rather than the attractiveness of the centers of their respective downtown areas. Tourists are attracted to the two cities' commercial attractions (themed amusement parks and gambling casinos) rather than the urban, commercial, or civic features of their respective cities' centers.

MIX, MASS, AND MESH

Many proposed convention centers and other major downtown projects are rationalized in the name of synergy, the claim being that they will serve as a "catalyst" for revitalization of the central business district. City leaders would find it interesting to return to the dictionary meaning of this word, which has been used to justify the expenditure of hundreds of millions of dollars in public and private "mega" investments. A catalyst is defined as an agent or independent substance that causes an action between two or more different elements to create a new substance–in this case, the center city. Unfortunately, convention centers are frequently built in downtown areas with no existing "different elements"; that is, viable residential, commercial office, or retail concentrations. They are often inserted as a "silver bullet" or "magic charm" in a part of the city that has been unable to attract new private investment and are then expected to be a catalyst to success.

Considering the checkered history of urban revitalization schemes, it is important to understand what is required for a catalyst, as an agent causing a chemical reaction, to perform its function.

The catalyst must be placed in the presence of two or more existing different elements; for example, two existing and dissimilar types of urban activities.

The two or more existing elements must also be proximate or adjacent to each other and the catalyst before the catalyst (convention center) can cause the intended interaction or transformation of the area. The catalyst won't create the desired "new substance," or cause it to appear, if the other elements are not proximate to each other and to the catalyst.

To summarize, many redevelopment plans (and convention centers) fail because the essential number of different ingredients (the Mix) are not present at the same time, in the required quantities (the critical Mass), or they are not sufficiently proximate to each other (the Mesh) to enable the promised catalytic or synergistic reaction (the interaction) to occur. For example, the redevelopment programs in Boston, Baltimore, and, most recently, San Diego have been enormously successful because the critical thresholds of occupied office space (employees), housing (residents), public transit, and retail shops/restaurants (visitors) were built in close proximity or were already in place to support the planned catalytic or synergistic change (Sagalyn & Freiden, 1991).

On the other hand, we can recall dozens of well-intentioned, albeit abortive, efforts to revitalize a center city area by building an aquarium, convention center, headquarters office building, five-star hotel, sports arena, or performing arts center–all piecemeal efforts that did not work because there was no mesh with other elements in the area and no commitment to add them. Sadly, in addition to the hundreds of millions of dollars that government (taxpayers) or business investors (stockholders) later realized were wasted, these projects harmed the credibility of future proposals to "jump start" the center city.

Given the requirement for mix-mass-mesh, the term "physical and economic linkages" is not an empty catch phrase. For example, the media recently reported that a major U.S. "gateway" city had its center city revitalization well under way because it had received final approval and funding for construction of a new performing arts complex, a sports arena, and a major owner-occupied office development. The newspaper article and local television failed to mention that these facilities were miles apart from each other, separated by acres of blighted and vacant commercial areas. Other center city transformations have been unsuccessful for the simple reason that two or more healthy elements were either beyond comfortable walking distance from each other or separated by a six-lane highway, an elevated highway underpass, a river, or some other visual–perceived or "virtual," albeit functioning–barrier.

The Metrics of "Attractiveness"

But how can a center city's attractiveness be quantified?

Fortunately, there are specific, quantifiable characteristics common to all (attractive and less-attractive) city centers that can be combined to form an accurate "yardstick" or predictive index to measure its relative appeal to professional associations (Petersen, 1985-1999) and institutional investors alike. ERE Yarmouth, an international real estate investment company, conducts annual surveys of hundreds of real estate developers and institutional lenders. These surveys reveal that many economically healthy and robust center cities are uniquely appealing to major commercial real estate developers and investors. These center cities are the only downtown areas consistently attracting long-term new construction and investment. For example, of the five top-ranked real estate markets (citywide) revealed in an annual survey of the largest real estate investors (Miller, 1996-2000), four are also top-ranked for downtown investment (Seattle, San Francisco, Boston, and Chicago). Not surprisingly, these cities are also top ranked for convention attendance. From 1996 to 2000, the 10 cities consistently ranked highest for real estate investment and new development were Boston, Chicago, Denver, Los Angeles, Minneapolis, New York, San Diego, San Francisco, Seattle, and Washington, D.C. (Miller, 1996-2000).

Although the authors of the ERE Yarmouth report do not quantify their defining criteria for a successful center city, they do cite what they have consistently observed to be the attributes these cities hold in common. Subsequent quantitative research conducted by the author has substantiated the validity of these five attributes and their correlation with center cities enjoying the highest levels of new investment and the largest numbers of attendees to the annual conventions of professional associations. At the same time, this research has revealed the essential "metrics"; that is to say, the scale or quantity of each required "attribute," the measurable "minimum specifications" for each condition. These are the critical metrics for the five essential attributes for a "24-hour center city" identified by the author's of the ERE Yarmouth survey: diversified tax base, security, access to mass transit, attractive and affordable housing, and nearby shopping. Cities ranking highest in these attributes are characterized in the ERE Yarmouth reports as being "24-hour cities," as compared to the downtown areas or centers of all the other cities in the largest markets which they termed as being either "9-to-5 cities" or "suburban agglomerations."

A Diversified Tax Base: One way to determine the heterogeneity of a center city's tax base is to start by selecting a single point; for example, the center of the commercial business district or a similar point in the center of the maximum concentration of high-rent, "class A," commercial office space, retail, or residential development. After identifying this central point, draw a circle to enclose all the development or economic activities–the Mesh–within a one-mile radius or a 15 to 20 minute walking distance. Tabulate the amounts– the Mass–of each type of development or activity–the Mix–in terms of residential population, dollar volume of retail sales, gross sales of restaurants or eating and drinking establishments, total occupied "class A" office space, number of full-service hotel rooms, and so forth. The results of these tabulations reveal much about the livability and diversity of activities in this area.

For example, a one-mile radius within downtown Spokane, certainly not one of the 20 largest markets of the United States, encompasses nearly 20,000 residents and includes retail establishments and restaurants with annual sales exceeding $200 million. When we compare Spokane's center city's concentration of activities to the level of economic activity and residential population within a similar radius of the centers of several much larger cities (that is, those city centers within the nation's largest, top 20 metro areas–those areas the federal government terms "metropolitan statistical areas" or MSAs), we discover that 10 of the centers in these cities have fewer residents or lower retail sales than Spokane.

The essential critical Mass for each of the required economic activities (the Mix) in the center of a major city is the following: occupied "class A" office space exceeding three million square feet, retail plus restaurant sales of more than $200 million, and a permanent residential population of 20,000 or more. (See Table 1)

Security: Concern about personal safety is always identified as a deterrent to new investment in downtown areas and to convention visitation, as well. The ERE Yarmouth surveys did not fail to report this. The author's research obtained the crime rate for areas of the same size within the downtown areas of each of these MSAs. Calculating the crime rates for these areas, circumscribed by a one-mile radius, is a more reliable index of personal safety in the center city than crime rates within the entire city, or the "downtown" area, as reported by the federal government. This is because the "downtown" areas, as defined by the federal government, vary in size from city to city.

Of these MSAs, the 14 with center city populations exceeding 20,000 residents and retail sales exceeding $200 million also report the lowest crime rates: .86 to 6.8 per thousand residents (and one at 8.0) for an average of 3.4. In comparison, the 10 cities with resident populations and retail sales of less than 20,000 and $200 million, respectively, exhibit the highest crime rates. Of these 10 city centers with lower population and retail sales within the one-mile radius, three had rates above 11.0, with an average among the 10 of 8.9. In other words, these 10 cities had crime rates more than double the average of the crime rates for the 14 city centers with higher residential populations and retail sales. It is interesting to note that Chicago and New York were among the cities with the lowest crime rates within their centers, both with 1.7 crimes per thousand residents within the one-mile radius.

TABLE 1. Vital Signs of 26 Major U.S. Cities

CENTER CITY	CBD Class A Occupied Office Space (MILLION SQ. FT.)	Percentage of Work Trips Transit	Percentage of Work Trips Walk/Bike	Crimes Per 1,000 Residents	Retail Sales (Millions)	Population (000)
				(ONE MILE RADIUS OF CENTER)		
ATLANTA	11.0	16%	17%	8.70	$194	13.6
BALTIMORE	7.9	20%	26%	3.20	$216	34.0
BOSTON	23.2	48%	53%	3.00	$334	37.8
CHICAGO	41.8	61%	63%	1.70	$428	49.0
CINCINNATI	6.7	17%	18%	2.50	$339	24.9
CLEVELAND	9.2	21%	23%	5.50	$78	7.4
DALLAS	18.3	9%	10%	19.10	$74	5.3
DENVER	12.0	17%	20%	5.50	$186	14.3
DETROIT	2.3	10%	12%	5.70	$120	15.1
HOUSTON	21.8	16%	17%	14.60	$111	8.7
LOS ANGELES	50.5	14%	17%	5.80	$305	37.8
MIAMI	4.5	12%	13%	8.0	$348	33.8
MINNEAPOLIS	12.9	24%	28%	1.80	$396	26.8
NEW YORK	186.8	74%	81%	1.70	$2,220	157.0
PHILADELPHIA	30.2	44%	51%	2.50	$369	60.6
PHOENIX	7.4	5%	7%	6.25	$138	13.6
PITTSBURGH	12.8	33%	35%	2.66	$144	13.9
PORTLAND	7.7	17%	21%	3.40	$254	21.8
SAINT LOUIS	6.0	10%	12%	9.40	$101	12.4
SAN DIEGO	4.9	12%	15%	6.80	$272	28.5
SAN FRANCISCO	33.6	50%	56%	0.86	$1,028	106.0
SAN JOSE	2.5	NA	NA	1.80	$510	36.7
SEATTLE	13.1	14%	26%	1.50	$492	39.3
SPOKANE	0.9	4%	8%	7.10	$211	19.0
TAMPA	3.7	2%	4%	11.40	$98	8.7
WASHINGTON, D.C.	9.5	39%	44%	2.70	$406	47.3

Sources: Office Space: Isabell & Silverwright, 1998; Public Transit Use: *County and City Data Book, 1994*; Crime Rate, Retail Sales, and Population: Claritas, 1997.

Access to Mass Transit: The ERE Yarmouth authors, after reviewing a decade of investor surveys, concluded that access to mass transit is also a critical need for the center city. Again, corroborating this conclusion, the research demonstrates that the percentage of city workers using public transit closely correlates with the city centers most attractive to institutional real estate investors.

If fewer than 10% of center city workers use mass transit, this tends to indicate a "9-to-5" downtown, which is less attractive to major real estate investors. For example, only 2 of the 14 "most attractive" city centers had public transit ridership below 10%. In comparison, the European city of Helsinki reports that a whopping 70% of its population relies on public transit to commute to the city center during rush hour (Perkkiö & Radoviç, 1996). Similar high rates of transit ridership are common in major cities throughout Europe.

Attractive, Affordable Housing: ERE Yarmouth's observations also revealed that the availability of attractive, up-scale housing is as important as the affordability of housing for a successful center city. No "investor-friendly" center city has a resident population of less than 20,000 within a one-mile radius of its center.

Nearby Shopping: A residential population of less than 20,000 indicates insufficient support for a supermarket. Similarly, the total annual retail and restaurant sales (within the one-mile radius) must exceed $200 million for a center city to become a "retail destination" capable of attracting the patronage of suburban residents, downtown workers, and out-of-town visitors.

MEASURING ATTRACTIVENESS: FIVE ESSENTIAL ATTRIBUTES

These five critical attributes or features have been quantified for the area within a one-mile radius of the center of the downtown area of each city. The data is shown in Table 1. Importantly, the cities ranking highest in each of these five attributes (quantified as shown in the table) are nearly identical to the list of cities enjoying the highest annual attendance to meetings of professional associations in their convention centers. These same cities have the highest concentration of center city hotel rooms and have consistently ranked highest in the ERE Yarmouth surveys of real estate investors and lenders.

Only one city named in the ERE-Yarmouth "top markets," Denver, is not ranked highest by the five center city attributes. Denver's center city population was slightly less than the critical Mass of 20,000; however, it has been growing rapidly (especially in the new neighborhood development on the center city's western edge) and may (by 2005) already exceed the 20,000 level. Conversely, one center city ranks among the top 10 in terms of the five critical attributes, Philadelphia, but is not ranked among the institutional investor's top 10 based on the ERE Yarmouth surveys. It should be noted that Philadelphia's ranking has improved each year from 1996, when it was 17th, to 2000, when it was 13th, and has been recognized by the author of a more recent ERE Yarmouth report as the "come-back city."

ADDITIONAL CRITERIA

Further study of the comparative statistical data for the 24 largest cities' centers reveals other quantifiable characteristics of the most attractive and successful.

Office Space: The most attractive centers contain a higher concentration of "class A" office space than any of the office sub-markets within their metropolitan areas.

Civic Uses: The most successful city centers are almost always the location for local and regional government centers, most major cultural arts and public assembly facilities (convention center, arena, performing arts theater), and large public parks and plazas.

Comercial Establishments: These centers also attract "up-market," one-of-a-kind restaurants and retail stores and have the highest concentration of "class A," full-service hotel rooms.

Validating "Mix-Mass-Mesh": Real Estate's Rules of Thumb

Closer examination and analysis of the most attractive cities' centers reveals other, albeit related, relationships and requirements needed to sustain and perpetuate these important districts. For example, one "class A" hotel room normally requires the demand (from business or "commercial" travelers) generated by 3,000 square feet of occupied "class A" office space. This volume (of commercial visitor demand) may be augmented by additional (albeit extraordinary) levels of demand created by leisure travelers or convention group visitors. It is worth noting that no hotel has ever achieved financial success by relying solely on convention visitors as the primary source of its occupancy.

Because 250 to 350 rooms represent an economically efficient size for a "class A" full-service hotel, it is commonly agreed among the new hotel development decision makers of the largest national full-service hotel chains that they will only consider sites in city centers with three million or more occupied square feet of "class A" office space.

If the high cost of parking in a center city business district would be a deterrent to attracting clerical workers (if these lower-paid workers had to depend solely on their automobile for their commute to work), public transit ridership greater than 10% may be the threshold level required to overcome this potential barrier to successful office leasing. This higher level of ridership may also be essential for a transit company to generate enough fare-box revenue to enable it to provide a frequent, clean, and comfortable level of service.

Center cities without three million square feet of occupied "class A" office space may be able to support a "class A" hotel (or two) if they can attract urban tourists, convention attendees, and other non-business oriented (commercial visitor) room demand (for example, San Jose or Spokane).

Without a critical mass of affluent residents, some successful center cities are able to attract unique specialty retail shops and "white table cloth" restaurants if they have one or more "anchors" or major pedestrian generators not duplicated elsewhere in the metro area. For example, an "up-market" or luxury department store, large university, state capitol building, major cultural attraction, or "destination entertainment" (that is, entertainment not found in the suburbs) may substitute for a high-income resident population. (San Antonio's "Riverwalk," Indiana's State Capitol building, or Seattle's "Pike Place Market" serve as prime examples.)

Convention delegates will avoid attending meetings in cities that do not offer a sufficient concentration of quality hotel rooms, restaurants, retail shops, and entertainment within walking distance of the convention center. In other words, professional associations do not want to meet in "9 to 5" cities or in cities that do not offer the unique urban amenities that will persuade them to meet in a center city rather than a resort or "edge city" location.

These and other findings emerge as we further scrutinize the data over time, correlate the analysis with other information, and continue to measure the levels of new private investment and convention attendance in all major city centers.

CONCLUSION

It is not reasonable to conclude from the evidence presented in this paper that an attractive or successful center city is essential or even feasible for all communities. The objective of this presentation is to demonstrate that in many cases the center city's preservation or revival efforts can only be cost-effective when the "Mix-Mass-Mesh" are in place. This is because they are a required prerequisite for preservation or revitalization efforts to succeed. Sufficient reliable data is readily available to define and measure the vital signs of a healthy center city. A single "silver bullet," or one-step panacea solution, has consistently proven to be a waste of the taxpayer's and investor's time, opportunities, and money because these "remedies" are not derived from the findings of empirical research or supported by historical evidence.

Regardless of the motives of business, governmental, or civic leaders' efforts to revitalize a downtown (whether driven by "corporate citizenship," a desire to increase convention attendance, to increase property values, or to create a safer environment for center city residents and employees), the evidence shows that all successful cities–those that enjoy high levels of city-wide new investment–also have prospering and attractive centers (Miller, 1996-2000).

If we believe that center cities are important, that they possess unique attributes and values unattainable elsewhere, we should acknowledge that their existence depends on more than simply satisfying its residential population. We must also recognize–and ultimately try to cure–the many negative conditions and forces that cause these areas to be unattractive to investors and potential convention attendees on whose spending our community's image as well as our tax base will depend.

REFERENCES

Claritas. (1997). *Claritas Demographic Report.* Claritas, 5375 Mira Sorrento Place, Suite 400, San Diego, CA 92121.

County and City Data Book, 1994. (1997). Based on U.S. Census data, 1994.

International Association of Convention and Visitor Bureaus. (1980, et. seq.). *Convention Delegate Spending.* Unpublished data for specific cities.

Isabell, T. W., & Silverwright, M. J. (1998). *Compass National Market Report.* Atlanta, GA: Compass Management and Leasing Inc.

Miller, J. D. (1996-2000). *ERE Yarmouth's Annual Survey Report.* New York: ERE Yarmouth.

Perkkiö, P., & Radoviç, R. (Eds.). (1996). *Helsinki Urban Guide.* Helsinki, Finland: Helsinki City Planning Department.

Petersen, D. C. (1985-1999). *Convention Industry Annual Report.* Tampa, FL: Horwath & Horwath International (1985-1990) and Price Waterhouse LLP (1991-1999).

Sagalyn, L. B. & Freiden, B. J. (1991). *Downtown, Inc.* Boston: MIT Press.

Index

BOOK ORDER FORM!

Order a copy of this book with this form or online at:
http://www.haworthpress.com/store/product.asp?sku=5326

Current Issues in Convention and Exhibition Facility Development

____ in softbound at $24.95 (ISBN: 0-7890-2598-1)
____ in hardbound at $39.95 (ISBN: 0-7890-2597-3)

COST OF BOOKS ____

POSTAGE & HANDLING ____
US: $4.00 for first book & $1.50
for each additional book
Outside US: $5.00 for first book
& $2.00 for each additional book.

SUBTOTAL ____

In Canada: add 7% GST. ____

STATE TAX ____
CA, IL, IN, MN, NY, OH & SD residents
please add appropriate local sales tax.

FINAL TOTAL ____
If paying in Canadian funds, convert
using the current exchange rate,
UNESCO coupons welcome.

❑ BILL ME LATER:
Bill-me option is good on US/Canada/
Mexico orders only; not good to jobbers,
wholesalers, or subscription agencies.

❑ Signature ____

❑ Payment Enclosed: $ ____

❑ PLEASE CHARGE TO MY CREDIT CARD:

❑ Visa ❑ MasterCard ❑ AmEx ❑ Discover
❑ Diner's Club ❑ Eurocard ❑ JCB

Account # ____

Exp Date ____

Signature ____
(Prices in US dollars and subject to change without notice.)

PLEASE PRINT ALL INFORMATION OR ATTACH YOUR BUSINESS CARD

Name ____

Address ____

City ____ State/Province ____ Zip/Postal Code ____

Country ____

Tel ____ Fax ____

E-Mail ____

May we use your e-mail address for confirmations and other types of information? ❑ Yes ❑ No We appreciate receiving
your e-mail address. Haworth would like to e-mail special discount offers to you, as a preferred customer.
We will never share, rent, or exchange your e-mail address. We regard such actions as an invasion of your privacy.

Order From Your **Local Bookstore** or Directly From
The Haworth Press, Inc. 10 Alice Street, Binghamton, New York 13904-1580 • USA
Call Our toll-free number (1-800-429-6784) / Outside US/Canada: (607) 722-5857
Fax: 1-800-895-0582 / Outside US/Canada: (607) 771-0012
E-mail your order to us: orders@haworthpress.com

For orders outside US and Canada, you may wish to order through your local
sales representative, distributor, or bookseller.
For information, see http://haworthpress.com/distributors

(Discounts are available for individual orders in US and Canada only, not booksellers/distributors.)

Please photocopy this form for your personal use.
www.HaworthPress.com

BOF04